The Essential
Anatomy of Britain

The Essential Anatomy of Britain

Democracy in Crisis

ANTHONY SAMPSON

LONDON   NEW YORK   SYDNEY   TORONTO

First published in Great Britain 1992

This edition published 1992
by BCA by arrangement with
Hodder and Stoughton Ltd

CN 1769

Photoset by Rowland Phototypesetting Ltd,
Bury St Edmunds, Suffolk

Printed in Great Britain by BPCC Hazells Ltd,
Aylesbury, Bucks, England
A Member of BPCC

Contents

Acknowledgments

In this my seventeenth book I am grateful to many of the usual suspects who have helped me through earlier books. They include my publishers, Hodder and Stoughton, specially my two editors Eric Major and Simone Mauger; my agent Michael Sissons of Peters Fraser Dunlop; and my assistant Carla Shimeld who has helped both to organise and to research. I am also indebted to the editor of the *Independent*, Andreas Whittam-Smith, for first encouraging me before the general election to re-inspect Britain's anatomy. As always I owe much to my wife Sally for advice, good judgment and proof-correcting. And as usual I am in debt to many friends as sources and spies who will prefer to remain nameless.

I am specially indebted to Robin Denniston, my old friend and first editor, formerly publisher of the Oxford University Press and managing director of Hodder and Stoughton. He has helped me to give shape and direction to the book with his unique editorial flair: without him the book would have been duller and the task less fun.

A.S.

Preface

This is a more personal and more concentrated book than my earlier versions of *Anatomy of Britain*, which I began thirty years ago in 1962. Like earlier *Anatomies* it offers an overview of the main centres of British power, who runs them and how they interact. This one also tries to show how they have changed over those three decades – a specially interesting time-scale as a more commercial generation comes to power with no memories of wartime, while having to confront many problems which seem to recur in a roughly thirty-year cycle.

But this book, as its title suggests, focuses more sharply on essential crisis points: particularly the weakening of democratic representation which accelerated during the eighties, which has affected nearly all the power-circles, and which is still more evident in the wider context of Britain-in-Europe. The democratic crisis shows itself also in commercial areas where decision-making has been taken over by a few groups and people, most visibly in the highly-centralised media which condition many people's attitudes to life. While businesses claim to offer the consumer greater choice, major decisions are taken by a tiny group of people, and shareholders' representation is now threatened as much as the voters'.

This is not a book about politics; and I depict the political parties only as part of the larger pattern of power, control and ownership. Nor can it pretend to be comprehensive: I do not try to cover the complex workings of welfare, or the role of such professions as solicitors, accountants or doctors who are crucial and controversial, but not part of the central power-structure. I have concentrated on those overlapping circles which most clearly determine the future character of the country.

I offer the reader a personal tour of the power-circles, using occasional descriptions of typical scenes to convey the atmosphere and feel of areas of power, followed by accounts of the workings and realities which lurk beneath the façades.

The tour pursues what seemed to me a natural trail of interlocking power-circles. The first part begins with the watershed of the 1992 general election and the new parliament and political leadership which it caused. This leads on to the changing patterns of the Civil Service, the law and the special current crisis of the monarchy. It concludes with the effects of the educational system on the class structure, and the most obvious sufferers from that: the scientists and engineers who are at a clear disadvantage in comparison with continental Europe.

The second part moves to the agglomerations, upheavals and scandals in finance and insurance, and the predicament of industrial managers and small businessmen in a country dominated by powerful corporations; concluding with the most influential wielders of concentrated power, the controllers of the media.

The third part looks at the casualties of these trends during the eighties; first the workers, workless and homeless, including the voluntary travellers who now see their escape-routes and freedoms threatened; then the local councils, provincial cities and regions which have all seen much of their former autonomy disappear towards London.

As the tour progresses, it becomes less a tour of a self-contained island, more a tour of Britain-in-Europe; for the influence of European institutions and pressures is evident in almost every sphere. Many apparently purely British circles turn out to lead off the map, as the back cover of this book conveys, and I try to give some glimpses of how Britain looks from this wider perspective – whether from the parliament in Strasbourg, from the Channel Tunnel terminal, or from European cities.

Finally I show how the centralisation looks from the centre – from the viewpoint of the prime minister in Downing Street – before trying to sum up my own concerns about the weakness of democracy in the thirty-year perspective. For I believe that Britain's anatomy now shows very serious deformities, which require urgent attention, and which can only be put right by much greater public protest and involvement – which are not yet much in evidence.

Even more than my earlier books, this has had to be written with speed, as the events and problems have unfolded; and I have tried to convey that sense of immediacy and closeness. In covering so much territory so quickly I realise that I have made some mistakes, and I will be grateful for any corrections which can rectify them in the following editions. But I make no apology for painting a very wide landscape in a short time; for I hope every reader will find it useful to look over the immediate hedges of institutions, parliamentary politics or financial market-places, on to the wide horizon of the nation and the continent which is affecting everyone's future.

Anthony Sampson, London
October 1992

The Essential
Anatomy of Britain

I

Elections

The English people believes itself to be free; it is gravely mistaken; it is free only during election of members of parliament; as soon as the members are elected, the people are enslaved; it is nothing. In the brief moment of its freedom, the English people make such a use of that freedom that it deserves to lose it.

Jean-Jacques Rousseau, *The Social Contract*, 1743

At the Savoy Hotel in April 1992 the owner of the *Daily Telegraph*, Conrad Black, was throwing an election party in the Lancaster Room, decked out with television screens and central tables loaded with lobsters. It was the traditional electoral rallying place of the Right where politicians, bankers and industrialists could celebrate their victory. But this time there was a special tension, for all through the three-week campaign the polls had predicted an end of the Tory majority; and the exit polls and the swing-ometer were forecasting an indecisive result, if not a Labour victory. As the first guests arrived at 11.00 p.m. they were far from celebrating: there was talk of Scotland routing the Tories, and of a hung parliament leading to another election in a few months. The few non-Tories present were expecting to enjoy the discomfiture. The financier Henry Keswick was railing against the editor of the *Financial Times* which had told its readers to vote Labour. Margaret Thatcher herself turned up looking regal, with her husband and son, to rally her old troops, some of whom wished she were still in command.

But soon there was cheering from the anxious clusters round the television screens as the first results showed Conservatives hanging on to their seats, and by midnight it was clear that the Conservatives were back in power for a fourth term. There was a palpable change of atmosphere, and relief. The rich were already richer, and the Greek playboy Taki explained that London would remain what he called 'the greatest tax haven on earth'. The Canadian host Conrad Black appeared centre-stage like a heavyweight champion surrounded by seconds, his editor Max Hastings and his favoured columnists Paul and Frank Johnson. The many American guests seemed unsurprised: the editor Clay Felker explained that all elections were now only about taxes. Mrs Thatcher left to go on to Lord McAlpine's party where her closer supporters were celebrating. The dedicated vote-counters Alan Watkins and Anthony Howard still sat together, glued to the television screen; but most of the guests forgot about the election, and the businessmen went back to talking business: it was the end of politics for another four years.

It was not all relief. Lord Weinstock of General Electric, who had seen socialist governments come and go, was not sure it was good news. Algy Cluff, the oil tycoon, was worried about the lack of an alternative party and the signs of Tory racism in Cheltenham. Many bankers and businessmen had most of their interests abroad and were not seriously affected anyway. Most journalists were too embarrassed by their wrong predictions to bask in victory. A few Tory intellectuals were actually hoping for a spell in opposition to give them time for developing more radical ideas. Some professional politicians expected the new government soon to be facing a dangerous economic crisis, which would eventually give Labour the ammunition to mount a devastating counter-attack. And many guests, as they left in the small hours, were bewildered by a political scene with no precedent in the twentieth century: a Conservative Party in power for a likely seventeen years, without effective opponents either at home or abroad.

I left the party feeling it marked the end of the Left–Right seesaw that I had watched since the Second World War. Free market capitalism was again enthroned, with no idea powerful enough to challenge it. The Labour Party had proved unelectable; the Liberal Democrats whom I had supported could not rally votes for higher taxation or closer involvement with Europe. It was like a return to the Edwardian age before the First World War – a golden age now made familiar by television dramas about languid young men driving to romantic country-houses full of respectful servants. Yet that age was never as serene as it looked through the mists of two world wars: it was already threatened by constitutional crises, by Ireland, suffragettes and the growing Labour Party. And today, behind all the celebration, there were plenty of causes of foreboding: the gathering

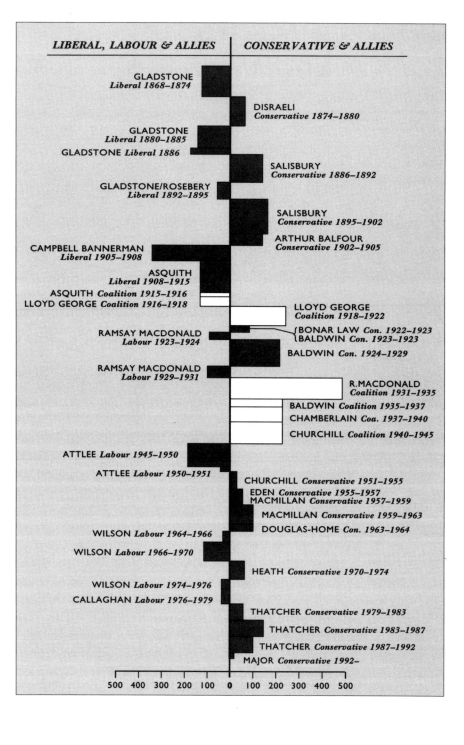

LIBERAL, LABOUR & ALLIES   CONSERVATIVE & ALLIES

GLADSTONE
Liberal 1868–1874

DISRAELI
Conservative 1874–1880

GLADSTONE
Liberal 1880–1885

GLADSTONE Liberal 1886

SALISBURY
Conservative 1886–1892

GLADSTONE/ROSEBERY
Liberal 1892–1895

SALISBURY
Conservative 1895–1902

ARTHUR BALFOUR
Conservative 1902–1905

CAMPBELL BANNERMAN
Liberal 1905–1908

ASQUITH
Liberal 1908–1915

ASQUITH Coalition 1915–1916
LLOYD GEORGE Coalition 1916–1918

LLOYD GEORGE
Coalition 1918–1922

RAMSAY MACDONALD
Labour 1923–1924

BONAR LAW Con. 1922–1923
BALDWIN Con. 1923–1923

BALDWIN Con. 1924–1929

RAMSAY MACDONALD
Labour 1929–1931

R.MACDONALD
Coalition 1931–1935

BALDWIN Coalition 1935–1937

CHAMBERLAIN Coa. 1937–1940

CHURCHILL Coalition 1940–1945

ATTLEE Labour 1945–1950

ATTLEE Labour 1950–1951

CHURCHILL Conservative 1951–1955

EDEN Conservative 1955–1957
MACMILLAN Conservative 1957–1959

MACMILLAN Conservative 1959–1963

WILSON Labour 1964–1966

DOUGLAS-HOME Con. 1963–1964

WILSON Labour 1966–1970

HEATH Conservative 1970–1974

WILSON Labour 1974–1976

CALLAGHAN Labour 1976–1979

THATCHER Conservative 1979–1983

THATCHER Conservative 1983–1987

THATCHER Conservative 1987–1992

MAJOR Conservative 1992–

500 400 300 200 100   0   100 200 300 400 500

recession, the chaos in Eastern Europe, the growth of the underclass. Britain was now sailing into uncharted seas.

THE PENDULUM

There were clear dangers about a single party staying in power for two decades. The British democratic system, a model for so many others, has depended on what the Victorian prime minister Lord Salisbury had called 'the great law of the pendulum'. Only at election time – as Rousseau recognised – did British electors wield any real power to achieve change. Was this one moment of choice being removed as Britain came to be governed by a single ruling party like the Japanese? The question worries not only the opposition but many Conservatives who believe passionately in the freedom of choice, political as well as economic. As one of them, Samuel Brittan, put it: 'There was always a paradox in those who proclaimed a belief in freedom wanting one person to remain in power for ever and ever, and to amass more and more centralised power.'

There have been earlier scares about a one-party state, most notably in the early sixties – when I first tried to scan Britain's anatomy – when Labour had lost three elections in a row. Richard Crossman, the socialist theorist, reckoned that since universal household suffrage began in 1884 there had been an inevitable long-term trend towards Conservatism. 'In the course of the seventy-five years up to 1959,' he wrote, 'there have been only two left-wing governments with outright majorities.' But Hugh Gaitskell, the Labour leader, saw Britain more as part of a western trend, and insisted that western prosperity was favouring any party in power: 'governments in most countries in this last decade,' he told me i n 1961, 'whether of the Right or the Left, have found it pretty easy to stay in power.'

In fact the political moods were more international than they appeared to most British voters at the time. The election of President Kennedy in 1960 threatened the old guards across Europe; and Harold Wilson made the Tory government look tired under Macmillan and Sir Alec Douglas-Home. British voters were disillusioned with government rather than enthusiastic for the opposition; but they gave Labour a small majority in 1964, which they converted to a hundred with a brief boom in 1966. Soon it was the Conservatives who were afraid that the pendulum had stopped, and talked of Britain becoming a permanent social democracy like Sweden.

[4]

But public opinion all through Europe was already moving against equality and trades union power, which helped Ted Heath to his Tory victory in 1970.

In the seventies all pendulums began swinging more madly, as the oil crisis helped to topple European governments, including the Conservatives in Britain and Social Democrats in Sweden; and inflation continued to undermine any sense of stability. But by the late seventies the movements were becoming more synchronised, as the major western nations were swinging back to the right, towards privatisation and tax cuts. Even in France, where President Mitterrand still headed a nominally socialist government, he was compelled to liberalise and deregulate the economy to attract capital. The British Left took some time to realise that the western political landscape was being transformed more drastically than at any time since the Second World War; while the Conservatives were not much interested in European parallels. It was not until the late eighties that the common trends emerged more clearly in Western Europe, with the collapse of the Eastern Communist states and the discrediting of socialism. The long triumph of the Right in the eighties showed a deeper disillusion with social programmes than previous swings. Democrats in America, socialists in Britain and Social Democrats in Germany all looked to each other in vain to find a way back into power.

In the nineties the European Conservatives were all facing unexpected problems, as the Iron Curtain lifted to reveal the disappearance of their bogeyman and the full chaos in Eastern Europe and Russia. No one had foreseen the full implications of the reunification of Germany – which Mrs Thatcher had first opposed. The Bonn government, having refused to raise taxes when they first absorbed East Germany, faced far greater costs than imagined, and had to borrow on such a scale that it pushed up interest rates everywhere. All Western Europe found itself paying for the rebuilding of East Germany, which would soon be strengthening the German industrial base.

Meanwhile the West plunged into a prolonged recession, and Conserva-tive governments forgot the peace dividend and maintained arms pro-duction as a means of employment. The old economic faiths, whether Keynesianism or monetarism, had collapsed, leaving governments to battle against inflation with no longer-term purpose. The western governments were collaborating closely in their economic policies; but with little social commitment to make them more acceptable to ordinary voters. The British were always more part of a broad western trend than they realised; but they were in a state of confusion about their relationship with Europe. They were locked into other European economies, particularly the German; yet reluctant to become part of the political system.

EUROPE AND THE ELECTION

The election campaign of April 1992, even more than earlier campaigns, had obliterated most important issues – the environment, Northern Ireland, immigration, or world peace – because the main parties either agreed, or were both embarrassed by internal disagreements. The most glaring omission was Europe, on which much of Britain's future depended. It was a tragically missed opportunity to educate the British public, but it was obvious why it was left out. Both parties had almost torn themselves apart with their arguments about Europe. Labour had moved from being anti-European to pro-European in a few years, to the fury of the remaining anti-Europeans. Mrs Thatcher's hostility to the Community had compelled first Nigel Lawson then Sir Geoffrey Howe to resign, and precipitated her own downfall; but a year later her successor John Major faced his first major crisis by approving the modified Treaty of Maastricht in December 1991. It was hardly surprising that neither party put Europe on the agenda during the election.

Less than two months after the election was all over, Europe was back on centre-stage. The result of the Danish referendum threw the Conservatives into new turmoil and doubt about the Community. Ironically the Danes whose main interest in the Community had been selling cheese suddenly emerged as the champions of European democracy, and reminded the British people that they had been told almost nothing about the terms of the Maastricht Treaty.

There was nothing new about this ignorance of Europe. Like others who have tried to follow Britain's relations with the Community, for over thirty years I have been puzzled by this slow waltz towards the continent, advancing, retreating and moving sideways. Since Britain first applied for entry into the Community in 1962 governments had always moved by stealth. Macmillan himself had sidled into negotiations with his usual ambiguity, never prepared to weaken his American links, or to reveal that the Community was a political as much as an economic organisation. He never spelt out the implications of the first sentence of the Treaty of

[6]

Rome: 'determined to establish the foundations of an ever closer union among the European peoples.' Harold Wilson when he tried again in 1967 was still less prepared to come clean about it. When Ted Heath eventually joined Europe in 1972 he was fully committed, at a time when the Community was prepared for a new push to unity, including a common currency and foreign policy: but the next year the oil crisis and the surge of inflation divided the Community again, and soon swept Heath himself out of power. Only the subsequent Labour government, in its referendum in 1975, actually put the question of European membership to the people – 67 per cent of whom said yes – but without throwing much light on what it meant. And it was only in the late eighties that Labour became a predominantly pro-European party. Yet the workings of the Community were slowly but ineluctably transforming not only diplomacy and economic policies, but the basic structure of business, the environment and the Law.

In this broader context the British general election looked more like a local election for councillors who were allowed to discuss traffic or drainage while the big decisions were taken somewhere else. The political parties were engrossed in their personality contests, reported excitedly by Press and television; while observers from outside the island watched the political geography changing under their feet.

So it looked from Germany, where I happened to be on a lecture tour during the election campaign. The German audiences could not understand why British voters were so obsessed by one girl's operation for her ear. In Heidelberg a political scientist who specialised in British democracy showed me a paper explaining that the competition within the traditional two-party system was ill-adapted to national problem-solving or long-term analysis and planning. The Germans were themselves much concerned by the problems of Maastricht and monetary union, which were already giving them second thoughts: and they were baffled that British politicians appeared to have forgotten about them. And in East Germany I first understood the full implications of reunification. After the Bonn government failed to increase taxes to pay for it, they borrowed so heavily that all western Europe was paying higher interest-rates.

AMERICA AND EUROPE

Certainly the British were now more pro-European in one respect: they were less pro-American. In the early eighties Mrs Thatcher's policies had been profoundly influenced by American examples, whether in deregulating, denationalising, extending free enterprise or cutting taxes. And the British Conservatives, like the American Republicans, had rallied the more prosperous to vote against more public spending and taxes.

But through the eighties the British were increasingly worried by American political trends, and today neither Conservatives nor Labour look across the Atlantic for solutions to social problems as they did in the fifties or sixties. Rather they find lessons on what to avoid, including a growing underclass, disintegrating cities and the flight to suburbia which are less tolerable in the more crowded landscape of Europe; while for their industrial models they look to Japan rather than the United States. For many Britons the American dream is beginning to turn into an American nightmare.

Instead the British look more towards Europe for social models: whether to German welfare, French public transport or Dutch housing. In spite of the conspiracy of silence during the election, the political influence of Europe has been growing. On the Left, Labour leaders and trades unionists begin to see the Community as a more promising structure for fairer deals and better relations between capital and labour. On the Right, bankers and international businessmen see their future in an open European market place with a common currency and watch the Bundesbank more closely than the Bank of England.

But they cannot look to Europe for new models of democracy. The Europeans are looking back to the British, who are facing their own crisis of democracy, on three separate fronts. First, the continuation of a one-party state has severely weakened the choice of the voters, and made civil servants and others more dependent on a single set of ideas. Secondly, the political system became far more centralised in the eighties, as the Thatcher governments concentrated power on London and the Treasury, and diminished local and regional counterweights and alternative centres of influence, including the universities.

Thirdly, Britain has become more dependent on decisions in Brussels and Europe, with no accompanying democratic oversight or control. The processes of 'ever closer union' have become still more remote from the public participation or understanding, as the revolt against Maastricht revealed. And now in the midst of recession the British are locked into the strict discipline of the Exchange Rate Mechanism, about which most people know nothing.

These three problems of democracy – the centralisation, the one-party government and the lack of European democracy – will recur through the following chapters about the British political system. And they are all to be seen in the central forum of democracy, the mother of parliaments.

2

Parliaments

Never has the House of Commons been more publicised and popularised, with the help of the cameras. After their thirty-year rearguard action against television members of parliament soon realised that the cameras boosted their fame, while television news producers discovered a form of vox pop to represent the voice of the nation, and a political version of courtroom drama. Parliament offers a far better stage than the German Bundestag or the United States Congress, for as Walter Bagehot said, 'government by a club is a standing wonder'; and viewers can enjoy eavesdropping on this intimate club of outspoken individuals, far more disorderly and spontaneous than Congressmen or deputies. The despatch-box, the mace and the Speaker's throne provide hallowed props; calls to order or waving order-papers provide familiar rituals; while a new parliament can supply a fresh storyline or a twist to the plot, like the first woman Speaker, or the come-back of a white-haired ex-prime minister as father of the house.

Televised parliament achieved a new immediacy with the fall of Margaret Thatcher in 1990: beginning with the long, deadpan speech of her assassin, Sir Geoffrey Howe, climaxing with the amazing two weeks in November when Conservative members of parliament rose in revolt and ditched their leader with a ruthlessness that astonished other democracies, and ending with Mrs Thatcher delivering her unrepentant finale: 'I'm enjoying this.' And it was authentic history; for that parliamentary revolt rather than the general election turned out to produce the nation's new leadership and direction. Politics, which had been coming always closer to television, now seemed hardly to exist without the screen.

The House of Commons has never been quite as dramatic since Thatcher's departure. But Prime Minister's Question-Time every Tuesday and Thursday still shows the batsman facing the fast bowling. John Major cannot hit them for six like Margaret Thatcher, but he pops up and down holding his folder with some of the zest of the sportsfield.

The whole spectacle conveys the grand simplicity of British democracy, which is replayed after each general election. The newly-elected members of parliament converge from their constituencies all over the country, to represent the people who have chosen them, and to vote on their behalf. The intrigues and rivalries inside and outside the chamber provide the stage, not just for the cameras but for parliamentary reporters, commentators and sketch-writers who flourish as never before.

But the House of Commons is not quite what it looks. Just when the chamber is reaching a new peak of fame, its power is oozing further away: not just in familiar directions, towards Whitehall, the party-managers and fixers, but towards more distant centres of power in Brussels, Luxembourg or Strasbourg. Anyone who tries to report on Britain knows that whenever power appears to come out in the open, it turns out to have moved somewhere else. Parliament as the oldest political theatre of all has a long experience of concealing its loss of importance.

It looks very different without the cameras. Many speeches are so boring that members leave in droves; and the chamber often cannot provide the quorum of forty. And while the cameras convey a rip-roaring freedom of speech, the party discipline sets harsh limits on the outspokenness of these six hundred people, which became harsher during the eighties.

Mrs Thatcher came to power as the champion of individualism in parliament as elsewhere: 'I've always regarded individualism as a Christian mission,' she told me before she became prime minister, and poured scorn on modern members of parliament who showed 'followership' instead of leadership. But as prime minister she demanded extreme loyalty from her members of parliament which forced them into followership. Her own dominating style, magnified by television, discouraged dissent. At her peak she treated parliament as a foil for her solo performances, while humiliating whingeing ex-ministers on the back benches. Her most consistent and outspoken critic, Ted Heath, could still fill the House of Commons with his outbursts; but he lost most of his supporters as they waited to join Thatcher's government. Only one minister ever consulted Heath over the whole decade: John Major.

The new prime minister in theory welcomed more freedom of speech; but in practice he did what he could to prevent it, all the more when he was returned with a narrower majority of twenty-one. He made just as much use of the government's two gruesome weapons against potential rebels: the guillotine and the whips. The guillotine cuts down debates by allocating a fixed time for discussing a new Bill. It fell sixty-eight times

during Mrs Thatcher's eleven years, compared to twenty-one in the five previous Labour years: and under Major it is falling still more frequently. As
the rebellious Tory member of parliament Richard Shepherd complained to
me: 'It's part of the new coarseness of the parliamentary process.'

The whips, the party policemen who press members to vote for the
government, have a much longer history, and members exchange horror
stories of rough treatment by former chief whips. They hold the keys to
promotion and favours, ranging from free trips to knighthoods or jobs in
the government. And as fewer members have independent means or jobs,
still fewer can resist the lures of office. The Tory whips became more
dreaded and effective under Thatcher: they could compel members of
parliament with their three-line whips to stay up late at night, to prevent
the opposition laying an ambush to deprive the government of a majority.
When Major took over, members of parliament hoped for a freer regime,
but the whips are even tougher under their chief Richard Ryder, Major's
close ally; and when they lost patience with the rebel member of parliament Nicholas Winterton they sacked him from his chairmanship of the
Select Committee on Health – a new degree of vengeance. The whips
faced a greater challenge from the sixty-three new Tory members of parliament who were cockier and less respectful than earlier intakes: many of
them were 'Thatcher's children' with a strong dislike of Europe. But they
were also even more ambitious to join government; and the whips' real
secret is that their side of parliament, after thirteen continuous years, has
become an annexe or waiting-room to the government. And once in
office, parliament looks much less important. 'It wasn't until I joined
government,' said one just-retired minister, 'that I realised just how irrele-
vant parliament was.'

Members of parliament are less able to criticise and scrutinise the flood
of legislation. The Committees which are supposed to provide the scrutiny
look imposing enough. But most of their sessions are simply formalities,
where ministers recite their briefs and opposition spokesmen make routine
objections before the Bill is passed; and the process becomes still more
routine after a long period in power. As Ferdinand Mount describes it:
'Only a somewhat shamefaced conspiracy between the two front benches
and the parliamentary press lobby prevents the scandalous spectacle of
Committee proceedings being more fully brought home to us.'[1]

[1] Ferdinand Mount: *The British Constitution Now*, Heinemann, London, 1992, p. 162.

The House of Commons still presents a picture of variety and individuality. But as Thatcherism is succeeded by Majorism the power of party discipline and loyalty becomes clearer: as ardent Thatcherites remember that they had always had deep misgivings, and no one turns out to have supported the Poll Tax. And Britain's claim to have the most vigorous parliamentary democracy looks more doubtful. In the words of Professor Sam Beer, the veteran American student of British politics:

MP for MP, the British people are abundantly represented in the House of Commons. A rich diversity of ideas and interests is already there. Partisanship, however, distorts its expression and party control stifles its effectiveness. Release of this diversity by a little less British order and a little more American chaos could do wonders toward moving the Constitution further toward being a government by the people and, who knows? also further toward being government for the people.[2]

THE SERPENTS

Behind the public debates of parliament the hidden pressures on government influence legislation much more than speeches. Growing numbers of members of parliament are themselves well-paid to represent commercial or special interests, sometimes more assiduously than their own constituents. But the most powerful lobbies, like the big corporations or the Institute of Directors, do not bother much about members: they can go straight to ministers and civil servants. The ministers like to conceal the fact that they are influenced by these secretive meetings; but lobbyists can be much more persuasive than members, particularly if they represent major donors to the Conservative Party: and they have more patient long-term objectives which can steadily wear down ministers. They reach their annual climax when the Chancellor of the Exchequer is preparing his budget, and receives petitions from business interests pressing for tax concessions. The interests of producers – centralised, close-knit and well-funded – inevitably win over the consumers who are scattered and fragmented; and the most powerful pressures of all, like the road-and-car lobby, change the face of the country through backstairs pressures which

[2] Lecture to the British Political Studies Association, Belfast, April 6, 1992.

are concealed from any public debate. Gradually non-commercial lobbies have also become much better organised, including major bodies like the Friends of the Earth or the Child Poverty Action Group, some with hundreds of thousands of paid-up members. Others relentlessly lobby members of parliament with mass-produced letters and deputations to intimidate and encircle them: as Douglas Hurd described them, 'like the serpents that came out of the sea to strangle Laocoön and his sons'. They have done much to counter big-business pressures with the help of effective publicity; but they cannot take account of grievances of the individual who can only appeal to his own member of parliament.

The most powerful serpents do not confine themselves to Britain, but intertwine all round Europe; and it is in Brussels not London that the most significant lobbying takes place. It is hardly surprising; from the beginning the Community provided a huge new opportunity for big banks and companies – particularly American and other multinationals who saw Europe emerging as a single market place like the United States. In its early days the Common Market was said to include seven powers – the six governments and Unilever. Now every major company has offices in Brussels, to maintain pressure on the European Commission and to keep track of each new regulation (and Unilever now has two rival lobbies, the Dutch and British arms, with different policies towards European union). Business lobbies bother little with the European parliament in Strasbourg. They go straight to the civil servants in Brussels who take the decisions, and who regard their lunches and entertainment as part of their way of life and self-image: 'I am lobbied, therefore I am.' And the non-commercial lobbies, particularly the Green pressure groups, have long ago realised that Brussels held the keys to protecting the environment or human rights. In 1980 they successfully lobbied for strict regulation of drinking water and bathing beaches throughout the Community which bypassed the national governments, and which eventually brought Britain to the International Court at The Hague for allowing polluted beaches.

THE ROAD TO EUROPE

Little of this comes within sight of the House of Commons, or the British public; for it belongs to a much wider stage and a long process which has been full of obscurities over the last thirty years. When members of parliament first debated joining the Common Market they did not know what they were deciding. 'Frankly, until we know what terms we can get,' said Harold Wilson, 'anyone who can claim to understand this issue in simple black-and-white terms is either a charlatan or a simpleton.' Fifteen years later, when Wilson was himself applying for entry, he preferred not to define the issue to parliament too clearly. When Ted Heath produced a White Paper about joining the European Community in 1971 it explained that there would be 'no question of any erosion of essential national sovereignty'. No one would have realised from reading the White Paper, as Anthony Lester has pointed out, that joining the Community would abridge the sovereign powers of parliament, enhance the powers of the judiciary and create support for a Bill of Rights (see Chapter 4).[3] When parliament eventually voted for the Treaty of Rome in 1972 it seemed to commit Britain to the 'ever closer union', but the process was stalled by the oil crisis; and Heath himself was surprised (he told me) by how little the Community had widened Britain's horizons. Mrs Thatcher, in spite of her hostility to the Community, asked parliament in 1986 to ratify the Single European Treaty which would abolish customs barriers by the end of 1992, under a system of majority voting. But while members of parliament voted for the Treaty they still saw it as quite separate from their national legislation; and it was not until the Treaty of Maastricht in December 1991 that European politics began to impinge more closely on Westminster.

Members of parliament are still barely equipped to understand, let alone control, the process of closer union. They spend only 5 per cent of their time discussing European problems. But of all Europe's legislators they have been most opposed to strengthening the European parliament. British members of the European parliament (MEPs) have been sitting in Strasbourg since 1972, and have been directly elected since 1979; but members in Westminster have treated them with disdain, making no use of their expertise and only recently allowing them limited access to the Palace of Westminster.

EUROPEAN PARLIAMENT

The European Parliament, whatever its limitations, remains the only instrument which can control or keep track of the Brussels bureaucracy; but it seems more than a continent away from Westminster. The journey

---

[3] Anthony Lester QC: *The Impact of Europe on the British Constitution*, 1992.

from London to Strasbourg is as expensive as to New York and can take almost as long, with few direct flights. The Palais de l'Europe which houses the parliament is certainly grand enough: a great square surrounding the circular chamber, full of restaurants, lobbies, committee-rooms and offices. But the building still has a hollow, alienated feeling and before long the whole institution will move to Brussels. In the courtyards are weird glass sculptures like giant test-tubes flowing with water, as if to emphasise that this is an international experiment. Members of the European parliament have the same pay as members of parliament in Westminster, with higher allowances and more efficient offices. But they still convey the expatriate's rootlessness, compared to the MPs' clubby sense of belonging in Westminster.

The central hemicycle is far more luxurious than the House of Commons, with a blue chair for each member, attentive waiters in morning coats and telephones in the aisles. It looks very supranational: the members are placed, not by nationality but by their European alignments, with socialists on the left of the podium and Conservatives on the right. The British Conservatives are now improbably joined with the European People's Party as the Christian Democrats now call themselves; but with their language problems they still find it hard to communicate with the other people in the party.

It was here in July 1992 that the British Foreign Secretary Douglas Hurd inaugurated Britain's Presidency of the Community at a dramatic time in Europe's history: the whole future of the Maastricht Treaty was in question, the Community was planning to take down its trading frontiers, and Yugoslavia was in chaos. But there was no dramatisation. Hurd spoke in his most superior mode, complete with hand-in-pocket, head-wobble and hand-lift, deploring the 'optimistic rhetoric which makes our citizens suspect us'. He commended the opening of frontiers and free movement of transport (with some tittering, since Strasbourg was at that moment blocked by French lorries on strike). He referred to the significance of subsidiarity and the need for quiet diplomacy. And he accepted the need for parliament to develop: 'our Community thrives on debate because we are all democratic.'

But he seemed shocked by the vigorous criticism which followed. 'You don't have the right to impose this concept of an *à la carte*, minimalist Europe,' complained the French socialist leader Jean-Pierre Cot: 'your concept of subsidiarity is fraudulent: you fail to have it on local and regional levels.' 'The Community needs a new lease of life,' said Willy de Clerq, the Belgian liberal, who went on to complain about John Major's minimalism. 'Your subsidiarity is perverse,' protested a Green German, Brigit Cramon-Daiber: 'subsidiarity means a federal Europe.' The sharpest criticism came from Winnie Ewing, the Scottish Nationalist who now belongs to the European Rainbow Party and who lashed into the secrecy of the Council of Ministers: 'Must all your proceedings be behind closed doors? Must we have this total secrecy?' Hurd replied to them all with headmasterly reproofs, warning his critics that last week's European Summit at Lisbon had shown a change of tide, against ceding national powers to the Community: 'You don't want to be left on the beach like a stranded whale.' And he repeated with relish: 'a stranded whale.'

It was a lively exchange, and at moments the European stage seemed to have become a reality as different nationalists argued across it. It was far livelier than the European parliament I had first seen twenty-five years ago, before Britain joined it, when the members seemed conscious of being in a provincial backwater and so glad to see any British journalist that they immediately invited me to a banquet. Now it had a more confident identity, at least among continentals, and the French regard it as a kind of House of Lords for retired Heads of State or ministers, including Giscard, Fabius and Cheysson.

But it was still a long way from being a real parliament, representing the plausible voice of any people; after two hours I found myself longing for some abusive demagogy from a Skinner or a Tebbit. Even at this peak-time the hemicycle was less than a quarter full. The Maastricht Treaty had shown up its limitations: for the lack of democratic supervision had been exposed not by members of the European parliament at Strasbourg but by the Danish voters. The national parliaments had been unable to keep track of their own governments' negotiations; but the European parliament was doubly removed from the real decisions as they tried to prise open what governments had already settled with each other at the Council of Ministers. Such international horse-trading, like all diplomacy, was inevitably at odds with democracy. The founders of Europe, including Jean Monnet, had hoped that the British would bring some robust democratic questioning and argument into the fray. But the British robustness was directed more at confronting other nations and scoring party-political points rather than questioning the secret agreements between ministers at the top.

It is hardly surprising that the European parliament should have so little impact on the British public, compared to the knockabout of Westminster. Douglas Hurd's speech and debate were unreported by most British newspapers, and not covered by television. As theatre the Strasbourg show is far too episodic, too full of unknown and unpronounceable foreign names, with no set-pieces like the budget speech, no rhetorical cricket like question-time, with which spectators can identify. Yet it is addressing much more fundamental problems. And only the European parliament can begin to understand and control the process which is integrating Europe's economies, impinging on key areas of British life and creating an international bureaucracy which is taking over powers from Whitehall.

3

Politicians and Cabinets

Whatever the limitations of parliament it provides the human material from which every government is formed; and most members are waiting to be offered one of the hundred government jobs. The prime minister cannot, like an American President, choose non-elected members for his cabinet, unless he makes them peers. The quality of government depends on the talent inside the two Houses of Parliament, from whom in turn are chosen the twenty-odd members of the cabinet – which remains the central link or buckle (as Bagehot called it) between the electorate and the executive.

The traditional notion of the cabinet as a committee was tested to the limit by Margaret Thatcher's eleven-year rule. She dominated her colleagues more completely than any other prime minister since the Second World War, dispelling the last lingering constitutional theories about the prime minister being 'first among equals', as she rejected consensus, appealed direct to her electorate on television, won three elections. Even Winston Churchill retained ministers he disagreed with and despised, like R. A. Butler, because they represented important strands of the party. Harold Macmillan was never strong enough to defy his own right wing, and he never recovered from firing a third of his cabinet in his 'night of the long knives' in 1962. Harold Wilson always had to conciliate his left, and to hold his government together by sleight of hand. Ted Heath kept on his rival Sir Alec Douglas-Home. But Thatcher from the beginning insisted on a cabinet of conformists; and any minister who contradicted her, except perhaps Whitelaw, fell through her trap door into the political dungeon.

'Looking back at ministers' memoirs of the sixties, it was a different world,' Sir Charles Powell, her Private Secretary for over seven years, told me: 'There was no risk of rebellion in cabinet, no sitting on the edges of chairs. Cabinet was never the stage for great debates or even wrangles. Her writ ran further down Whitehall than any prime minister since Churchill – or perhaps further.'

Number Ten became much more like a permanent court, with viziers and courtiers. The government was looking still more like an 'elective dictatorship', as Lord Hailsham called it in opposition, and closer to some kind of presidential system: but the British prime minister faced a weaker balance of power than the American President, and governed a much more centralised nation. By the mid eighties some senior civil servants were seriously worried that the constitution was threatened.

For almost ten years Mrs Thatcher could dominate cabinet and dismiss critics without serious risk. It was not until her Chancellor Nigel Lawson resigned in 1989 that she was more constricted, and only when her loyal colleague Sir Geoffrey Howe followed in 1990 was she seriously threatened. Even then, when she was at odds with most of the voters, and most Conservative members of parliament, she would not have been dislodged without the daring of Michael Heseltine.

The cabinet as much as the members of parliament finally undid her, as her former protégés told her she could not win the leadership election. Suddenly the cabinet system had come back to life, and the prime minister became again only one among equals. The Conservatives were able to de-stool their leader with the ritual ruthlessness of a primitive tribe, and to instate a more popular chieftain, John Major. To the consternation of Labour they could renew and re-form themselves in time for the general election. It was a historic achievement which suggested that British politics might be entering a new phase of one-party government which, like the Japanese LDP party, could change factions inside the party without letting in the opposition.

Was it really a new faction and a renewal? The leadership election was still under the long shadow of Mrs Thatcher. John Major was known to be her favourite – almost her invention. And he was much less combat-proven than earlier Tory leaders – except perhaps Sir Alec Douglas-Home in 1963. It was true that when Mrs Thatcher was chosen as leader in 1975, she had not run any great department of state. But she had shown her mettle as an opposition fighter with her own fierce beliefs. Major in his eleven years in the House had only known one party in power, and one leader; and he had spent only three years in the cabinet, mostly in the Treasury.

PRIME MINISTER

John Major's rise to the top was certainly a triumph of social mobility. He was the youngest prime minister since Lord Rosebery in 1894 (who lasted a year), with none of his privileges. The son of an ageing acrobat who had fallen on bad times, Major had lived in a semi-slum and had no money or qualifications when he left school at sixteen. He was briefly a manual worker, then unemployed: at twenty-three his longest journey had been to East Anglia.[1] Then he got his first steady job in the Standard Bank which sent him to Nigeria for two years and gave him a safe career.

But in political terms his career was ideal. In Brixton at sixteen he became a young Tory, when there was a backlash against Labour paternalism, and grasped politics from the street, with hard work, political sense and natural friendliness. Back from Nigeria in 1968 he was elected a councillor in Lambeth. By 1971 he was a Tory candidate for Holborn; by 1974 he was selected for a safe seat for life, in Huntingdon. It was a much easier ride to the House than for many rich young Tory candidates, with no serious setbacks.

In parliament in 1979 he was soon an obvious asset to Thatcherism and in less than two years was a parliamentary private secretary. Mrs Thatcher then picked him as an assistant whip, where he showed his political shrewdness and toughness; and by 1986 he was Junior Minister for Social Security. After the 1987 election he joined the cabinet as Chief Secretary, the most arduous job in the Treasury, where he was rigorous in cutting back spending, but was dominated by his Chancellor Nigel Lawson who set all the policy. Two years later, when Mrs Thatcher demoted Sir Geoffrey Howe, she made Major Foreign Secretary to strengthen him as her successor. But he only stayed there for three months before Lawson resigned and he took over as Chancellor, with his friend Norman Lamont as Chief Secretary. He was constantly battling against inflation, which was close to 10 per cent, and took the historic decision to bring Britain into the Exchange Rate Mechanism; but he was largely in the hands of the Treasury mandarins.

As Mrs Thatcher became more vulnerable he knew he was well-placed as successor: outwardly loyal to Thatcher but privately critical. His rivals

---

[1] Bruce Anderson: *John Major*, Headline, London, 1992, p. 45.

in cabinet, mostly the Cambridge crowd, knew they could not compete with the Brixton boy who had intuitive political sense and could attract crucial working-class votes. The Old Etonian candidate Douglas Hurd, aloof and defensive, only underlined Major's more open and outgoing style. The old guard, the 'men in suits', saw Major as the man of the people who would look after their interests, and saw Heseltine, who offered a real alternative to Thatcherism, as a dangerous maverick.

When John Major took over in November 1990 he soon relaxed the Thatcher autocracy. He allowed Hurd to run the Foreign Office, except during the Gulf War, and Lamont and the mandarins to run the Treasury. Number Ten became more like an office, less like a court: the staff were astonished to hear him casually ringing up David, Tristan or Jeffrey without any pomp. He gave short press conferences outside Number Ten and insisted on standing on a soap-box during the election campaign. Thatcher's long-lasting lieutenants Charles Powell and Bernard Ingham, who soon departed with knighthoods, were replaced with less assertive civil servants on shorter terms, Stephen Wall as Private Secretary and Gus O'Donnell as Press Secretary. And Major chose the open-minded Ambassador to Moscow, Sir Rodric Braithwaite, as his personal diplomatic adviser. Major quickly showed that the cabinet could still change back into a committee, to the relief of civil servants and ministers. He listened and conciliated between different views, with a chummy style almost opposite to Thatcher's. As Heseltine said: 'John sums up at the end of the meeting rather than the beginning.'[2] It was a return of a balance of power within the cabinet; for Major had acquired debts and obligations in his election.

But Major nevertheless inherited a much more centralised system than earlier prime ministers, with less idea of what to do with his power – as I discuss in the final chapter. It was not a return to the earlier leadership of Heath or Macmillan, who had both developed their own clear ideas in the years in opposition, and who in cabinet set their own course – whether retreating from empire or moving towards Europe. Major brought very little intellectual baggage that was not already labelled Thatcher; and for his political ideas he looked to the Policy Unit run by Sarah Hogg which soon became more influential.

Major is privately much more concerned about unemployment and hardship than Mrs Thatcher, and less sympathetic to businessmen; but

[2] The *Sunday Telegraph*, August 9, 1992.

he has not translated his concerns into alternative priorities and policies. 'To govern is to choose,' said the French prime minister Pierre Mendès-France: and by this definition Major has not yet governed. His career has been bounded by the immediate market place, of both politics or business: his greyness is part of his skill in reaching the top – offending no one, keeping options open. He has talked often about providing an agenda for the nineties, but it has not yet emerged; and his speech-writers notice that he is wary of long-term vision, or moral fervour. He is most emotional when defending the unity of the United Kingdom or fighting inflation: 'First and foremost,' he said in his first major speech as prime minister, 'I loathe inflation.'[3]

Major was inevitably a product of the party machine which had educated him, promoted him and set his perspective. His civil servants were struck by his intensely political viewpoint: he saw every problem instinctively in terms of votes, and avoided those in which there were no votes. Some were surprised by his choice of close personal friends – including David Mellor, Robert Atkins, Graham Bright or Jeffrey Archer (whom he soon ennobled); but in political terms they were useful.

He remains very party-political. Immediately after the election he emphasised that he represented not just Tory voters but the whole nation; but he has not yet made a clear transition to national leader. Many non-Tories expected him to widen the prime minister's patronage, and to break Mrs Thatcher's insistence on appointing 'one of us' to top jobs, committees or honours: they were encouraged when Lord Runciman, a past Labour sympathiser, was chosen to chair the Commission on Judicial Reform. But Runciman turned out to be the choice of the Home Office, suggested by the Attorney-General, Nicholas Lyell; and Major has since continued to favour Tories for honours and jobs – with the exception of Lord Owen, whom he has long admired, and whom he nominated as chief negotiator for the former Yugoslavia.

CABINET

It was not until Major won the 1992 general election through his own leadership that he could choose a cabinet more distinctive from Thatcher's. He produced a broader mix, promoting 'Wets' including Heseltine and

---

[3] December 4, 1990.

Waldegrave while adding the young right-winger Michael Portillo, and two women, Gillian Shephard and Virginia Bottomley. But they had nearly all owed their first promotion to Thatcher, who had provided their agenda and gave them little chance to develop their own popular appeal. Their success had depended on loyalty and efficiency while she provided all the rhetoric, inspiration and identity. Opposite are the twenty-two members of John Major's cabinet in October 1992. (Salaries unless otherwise stated were £63,047.)

It is a cabinet of graduates, ten from Cambridge, six from Oxford: only John Major and John Wakeham did not go to university. Like Ted Heath before him, Major looks like a classless totem surrounded by more class-bound followers. Most went into Tory politics at university, which remained their chief ambition thereafter, with their other job closely linked: the law and the City are the most popular careers. None went into industry. Four of Major's key supporters – Lamont, Gummer, Howard and Lilley – were all at Cambridge at the same time, three of them Presidents of the Union. They were politically formed by Cambridge in the early sixties, as earlier Tory and Labour cabinets had been formed by Oxford in the thirties – though in a less passionate mould, with a much more downbeat rhetorical style. But they went on to another kind of university: the Conservative Central Office and the research department which often provided useful employment for young Tories before they became members of parliament, including Chris Patten who was chairman of the party before the election – after which he lost his seat and governed Hong Kong. And Central Office, whatever its limitations, has become one of the most powerful party machines in the world, far better organised than the Republicans in the United States who follow their techniques: 'they're at least half a generation ahead of us,' said the Republican leader Newt Gingrich before the Convention in 1992: 'we're much more chaotic and decentralised.'

Most of the cabinet's careers have been confined to Britain, with little experience of the continent. David Hunt was at university in France, Gillian Shephard speaks French, Douglas Hurd was a diplomat in Rome; but others have seen little of Europe except on holiday. Michael Portillo – whose father fought as a Republican in the Spanish Civil War – is at pains to be thoroughly English.

Many have distinctive viewpoints. Sir Patrick Mayhew comes from an old Anglo-Irish family and always wanted to be in charge of Northern

Position	Holder	Age	Salary	Education
Prime Minister	John Major	49	£76,234	Rutlish School
Lord Chancellor	Lord Mackay	65	£106,000	George Heriot's School; Edinburgh and Cambridge Universities
Chancellor of the Exchequer	Norman Lamont	50		Loretto; Cambridge University
Foreign Secretary	Douglas Hurd	62		Eton; Cambridge University
Home Secretary	Kenneth Clarke	52		Nottingham High School; Cambridge University
Trade and Industry	Michael Heseltine	59		Shrewsbury; Oxford University
Transport	John MacGregor	55		Merchiston Castle School; St Andrews University
Defence	Malcolm Rifkind	46		George Watson's School; Edinburgh University
Leader of the Lords	Lord Wakeham	60	£50,558	Charterhouse School
Leader of the Commons	Tony Newton	55		Friends' School; Oxford University
Agriculture	John Gummer	52		King's School, Rochester; Cambridge University
Environment	Michael Howard	51		Llanelli Grammar School; Cambridge University
Wales	David Hunt	50		Liverpool College; Bristol University
Social Security	Peter Lilley	49		Dulwich College; Cambridge University
Citizens' Charter	William Waldegrave	46		Eton; Oxford University
Scotland	Ian Lang	52		Rugby School; Cambridge University
National Heritage	Peter Brooke	58		Malborough School; Oxford University
Northern Ireland	Sir Patrick Mayhew	63		Tonbridge School; Oxford University
Education and Science	John Patten	47		Wimbledon College; Cambridge University
Health	Virginia Bottomley	44		Putney High School; Essex University
Employment	Gillian Shephard	52		North Walsham School; Oxford University
Chief Secretary to Treasury	Michael Portillo	40		Harrow County Boys; Cambridge University

Ireland, which he now is. William Waldegrave alone comes from the tradition of Tory aristocrats, with Lord Cranborne, the future Lord Salisbury, waiting outside the cabinet. John Selwyn Gummer does not often forget that he is a canon's son. Malcolm Rifkind and Michael Howard are both influenced by their Jewish background: Howard once walked out of a dinner party when Israel was criticised. The Lord Chancellor comes from an austere Scots background, as a member of a strict little church; and four others – Lamont, Rifkind, MacGregor and Lang – have Scots roots.

But none has a political purpose or philosophy distinct from Mrs Thatcher's, with the exception of Michael Heseltine. He was the only member of her cabinet whom she feared and eventually the only one who dared to stand against her. With all his flashiness he has been remarkably consistent: supporting Europe, the environment, and intervention in industry which he can now practise at the Board of Trade. But he still keeps his options open, and awaits his opportunity to strike again.

The cabinet's experience is much narrower than thirty years ago, when the empire and two world wars had exposed politicians to very different societies, and emotions. Harold Macmillan, though he sentimentalised his past, *was* deeply influenced by the trenches and later by unemployment in Stockton. The young intellectuals who rethought policies in Conservative Central Office after the Second World War – Ian Macleod, Enoch Powell, Angus Maude, Reginald Maudling – were all influenced by wartime challenges and idealism. William Whitelaw was moved towards politics by his wartime task of writing letters to bereaved families. Lord Carrington, a major in the Guards, never forgot the sense of common purpose.

Through the fifties and sixties, Tory politicians were still harking back to Britain's past world role, and reluctant to face the workaday task of commercial survival. Now they have swung to the other extreme and retreated back to the island, from global statesmanship to domestic accounting. The road to the top lies not through the Foreign Office or Defence but the Treasury. Commercial realism was long overdue, but it began to overwhelm everything else including the European perspective in which much of Britain's commercial future must lie. The baby went out with the bathwater.

After over a decade in power any ruling party inevitably finds it harder to adapt, in Britain as in America; and has to wait for time in opposition to rethink its purpose. In office politicians become more complacent, preoccupied with the short-term. They accumulate vested interests, tolerate corruption, and confuse political purpose with a simple love of power. The replacement of Thatcher by Major brilliantly averted a Tory defeat at the general election; but it is not clear that it achieved a more fundamental shift than, for instance, the replacement of Macmillan in 1963 by Douglas-Home. There is now talk of a continuous one-party government with factions on the Japanese model. But the LDP in Japan has a more ruthless and corrupt system for maintaining power: its rival factions represent separate financial interests with backers in the background. In Japanese terms only Heseltine represents a different faction: Major so far represents a continuation of the Thatcher faction, with some loss of steam. And British democracy cannot easily be reconciled with a continuing one-party system which excludes the majority of the population.

OPPOSITION

The basic cause of the lack of choice is not the strength of the government, but the weakness of the opposition. Vigorous opponents become more important the longer a single party stays in power, whether to provide a future alternative or to keep the government honest and active. But the Labour Party suffered from a more serious malaise than the disillusion which afflicted all socialist parties in the eighties, as the tide turned against nationalisation and Communism. For in Britain Mrs Thatcher was able to attract working-class votes, including the unemployed, with her appeals to individualism, her attacks on the unions, her sale of council-houses – and her militant nationalism, against Argentinians and Europeans alike. And her triumph left Labour with a crisis of identity.

Neil Kinnock succeeded Michael Foot as leader in 1983 but could never quite recover that identity. He defeated his left-wing militants, and abandoned his old beliefs in nationalisation, high taxes for the rich and unilateral nuclear disarmament. But he was never a convincing convert to popular capitalism, while he seemed too anxious about appearing anti-capitalist, and too embarrassed by his party's links to Robert Maxwell, to effectively criticise the greed and inequalities of the eighties. What he could not provide was a convincing alternative programme; and only 35 per cent of the voters supported Labour in 1992.

His successor John Smith is shrewder, sharper, more pragmatic, the first lawyer to have led Labour since Attlee. He comes from a Christian socialist family in the West Highlands, joined the party at sixteen (like John Major) and at Glasgow University married a fellow socialist who remains more left-wing than him. John Smith became more flexible, admired Roy Jenkins, and stayed aloof from trades unionists except his Glasgow friend Gavin Laird. He joined the cabinet as Trade Secretary in 1978 at thirty-nine, just before Labour lost power; and in opposition he showed he could understand finance as shadow Chancellor. Perhaps he became too fascinated by it: during the 1992 election campaign he spelt out in painful detail the proposed Labour tax-increases – which helped to lose the election.

But Smith was well-placed to succeed Kinnock, supported by most of the unions and 91 per cent of Labour members of parliament. He quickly promised to abolish the union block vote and to woo women voters; Labour, he said, must rid itself of its 'macho style of debate'. He was helped by the elections to the national executive, which brought five women into the shadow cabinet, and a more flexible age-group.

The Labour leadership has changed its character more strikingly over thirty years than the Tories. All of John Smith's shadow cabinet have been to university, and none have the rugged origins of Frank Cousins, James Griffiths or Ray Gunter in Wilson's cabinet of 1964. But the tradition of Oxford dons who dominated Wilson's governments has also almost disappeared: there are now only two Oxford men – Blair and Meacher – and another two from the London School of Economics: most of the others studied in the north, Scotland and Wales. They are all affiliated with a trade union which often also helps to pay their election and office expenses; but most are otherwise aloof from the unions and are less the product of a party machine than the Tories. They are emphatically not London-based, and rich in Scots and northern accents. Their working experience is wider than the Tories, including a metallurgist, a forester and a ship's steward. But they lack the economic or financial expertise of the earlier Labour cabinets or the Tory cabinet. The two parties are more contrasted: a cabinet too interested in money faces a shadow cabinet not interested enough. These are the twenty-one members of the shadow cabinet in October 1992, after Bryan Gould resigned, with their shadow jobs, and affiliations or sponsorships by trades unions:

Shadow position	Holder	Age	Education and affiliation
Leader	John Smith	54	Dunoon Grammar; Glasgow University; GMB
Deputy Leader	Margaret Beckett	49	Notre Dame High; Manchester College of Science; TGWU
Treasury	Gordon Brown	41	Kirkcardy High; Edinburgh University; TGWU
Home Affairs	Tony Blair	39	Fettes College; Oxford University; TGWU
Trade and Industry	Robin Cook	46	Royal High; Edinburgh University; RMT
Employment	Frank Dobson	42	Holgate Grammar School; LSE; RMT
Transport	John Prescott	54	Grange Secondary Modern; Hull University; RMT
Chief Secretary to Treasury	Harriet Harman	42	St Paul's; York University; TGWU
Citizen's Charter and Women	Mo Mowlam	43	Coundon Court Comprehensive; Durham University; COHSE
Environmental Protection	Chris Smith	41	George Watson's College; Cambridge University; MSF
Wales	Ann Clwyd	55	Queen's School; University College, Bangor; TGWU
Education	Ann Taylor	45	Bolton School; Sheffield University; GMB
Foreign Affairs	Jack Cunningham	53	Jarrow Grammar School; Durham University; GMB
Development and Cooperation	Michael Meacher	53	Berkhamsted School; Oxford University and LSE; COHSE
Social Security	Donald Dewar	55	Glasgow Academy; Glasgow University; RMT
Health	David Blunkett	45	Tapton Mount; Sheffield University; NUPE
Environment (Local Government)	Jack Straw	46	Brentwood School; Leeds University; GMB
Defence and Disarmament	David Clark	53	Windermere Grammar School; Sheffield University; NUPE
Scotland	Tom Clarke	51	Columbia High; Scottish College of Commerce; GMB
Food and Agriculture and Rural Affairs	Ron Davies	46	Bassaleg Grammar School; University College of Wales; NUPE
Northern Ireland	Kevin McNamara	58	St Mary's College; Hull University; TGWU

Only a united opposition is likely to end the one-party rule, but that is John Smith's most difficult task; for it requires a pact with the heretics, the Liberal Democrats. When ten years ago a hundred ex-Labour supporters founded a new party, they believed Labour was pursuing a suicide course, anti-business, anti-nuclear deterrent and anti-Europe, and fatally dependent on the unions. Many of them (including myself) thought the new Social Democrat Party would either replace Labour as the main opposition party, or bring back Labour to its senses: and the new Social Democrat Party had a sensational take-off under the Gang of Four – Roy Jenkins, David Owen, Shirley Williams and Bill Rodgers. Eventually Labour recovered its sanity, while the Social Democrats were rent apart when they disagreed about merging with the Liberals. The Gang of Four retreated to the House of Lords or to America, and the merged party led by a Liberal, Paddy Ashdown, damages Labour more than the Conservatives.

But their policies have come closer to Labour's, particularly over Europe. In the 1983 election Michael Foot pledged to take Britain out of Europe within the lifetime of a Labour government. But Kinnock, having been anti-European, decided that withdrawal was both a vote-loser and economically self-defeating, and began to discuss common policies with continental socialists, while many of the unions (see Chapter 13) were also looking to a future in Europe. The elections to the European parliament in 1989 gave an unexpected boost to Labour, while showing up the Conservative rift. And by the late eighties John Smith was supporting the Exchange Rate Mechanism as the best discipline against inflation.

But Labour faces continental storms ahead. Like the Conservatives they never dared to properly explain Europe to their supporters, who are now tempted to blame the Exchange Rate Mechanism and the Bundesbank for high interest-rates and continuing recession. And Labour anti-Europeans like Peter Shore and Tony Benn are still lurking to attack the faceless foreign bureaucrats – who may soon include Neil Kinnock as a Commissioner in Brussels. The more Labour comes under attack over Europe, the more it will need to come closer to the Liberal Democrats.

But opposition can become a habit as corrupting and addictive as government, encouraging rival parties to attack each other more than their real enemy, and to enjoy short-term manoeuvres rather than long-term thinking. The real basis for a united opposition, I believe, must be a wider common cause, to create a fairer and more democratic society in both Britain and Europe. Within Britain, this book will suggest, the task is urgent: to balance the energy of private enterprise with dedicated public services; to shift priorities away from defence to education; to safeguard individuals against corporate power; to counter creeping centralisation with stronger and more representative local government; and to face up to the crisis of British democracy. As Shirley Williams put it a month after the election:

> The prerequisite of any new Opposition alignment has to be a wide-ranging movement for constitutional reform that embraces members of all parties and of none, voluntary organisations, churches, academics, trade unionists and business people – a modern reform movement on the scale of the great reform movements of the nineteenth century from which popular democracy emerged.[4]

4 *The Tablet*, April 18/25, 1992.

4

Bureaucrats

When parliamentarians go on holiday at the end of July, to reappear in October, they draw attention to the fact that the government and civil servants can do quite well without them. August and September, which saw the outbreak of both world wars, have long been dangerous months. August 1990 saw the invasion of Kuwait; August 1991 saw the Soviet coup; August and September 1992 saw a major economic crisis, and the commitment of British forces to Bosnia. Every summer-crisis produces talk of recalling parliament, which is usually rejected; but the invasion of Kuwait in 1990, and the collapse of the pound in 1992, brought members of parliament back from their holidays.

Members of parliament have never been well-equipped to control the executive: they have to rely on questioning the ministers who are responsible for the departments, and very occasionally confronting the senior civil servants in Select Committees. But the wall that separates the government from the rest has become higher as one party has remained in power; and in the meantime the bureaucracies become still more impenetrable, as they become more interlocked with bureaucracies abroad. In the eighties the Conservatives promised to 'roll back the frontiers of government'. But there is no sign that central government is weaker; and in several of its functions it has crossed over national frontiers. Key decision-making has receded further from public view, in meetings which thrash out deals and compromises well away from any parliament.

The fourth Conservative victory in 1992 inevitably changed the perspective of civil servants who prided themselves on their impartiality between parties. The run-up to the general election provided a greater test of that impartiality than any election since 1964. Senior civil servants were in a flurry of activity, talking with members of the shadow cabinet and writing 'what if?' papers which analysed how to implement the Labour manifesto. Even those who did not welcome a change felt some intellectual stimulus and challenge to present alternative ideas.

It never happened. There were some new ministers and some new ideas;

but no equivalent to the upheaval and excitement of 1964, or even 1970. There was no switch of patronage to encourage civil servants with other views, as the fourth term further entrenched the existing hierarchies. It was not just a party conformity; for the collapse of faith in socialism and nationalisation had anyway narrowed the area of dissent: civil servants were now nearly all capitalists, believing in the markets. But there were still many of them on the Left who privately believed in more financial regulation, more social conscience, or less privatisation; and they now felt still more forced into a single mould. With little prospect of political change, were they really different from politicians – or businessmen? 'When another party eventually gets into power,' as one of them said, 'they'll have a much harder confrontation with the civil servants.'

Mrs Thatcher had left Whitehall with a changed landscape. She was often accused of politicising or corrupting the civil service during the eighties, with much exaggeration. Few civil servants were promoted for purely ideological reasons: they were more favoured as 'can do' people who were efficient in execution – which had obvious benefits. But she was able to dominate government through sheer force of views and personality, and she was riding a tidal wave of public opinion, against nationalisation and regulation, more powerful than anything since the post-war wave ridden by Clement Attlee, in the opposite direction, to which civil servants had been equally loyal. But many civil servants certainly saw their service in a different light after Thatcher took over. Sir Antony Part was a Permanent Secretary who moved into business just before she came to power, and later (very unusually) wrote his memoirs. He reported that 'she took a distinctly closer interest in top appointments in the Civil Service than most of her predecessors had done. She was determined that anyone who filled a top post should be "one of us".'[1]

This power of patronage inevitably influenced civil servants' attitudes towards their profession. In theory their basic loyalty has always been to the monarch. In the words of their bible, the Code on Pay and Conditions of Service:

Civil Servants owe their allegiance to the Crown. In its executive capacity, the authority of the Crown is exercised through the Government of the day. Civil Servants are therefore required to discharge

[1] Antony Part: *The Making of a Mandarin*, André Deutsch, London, 1990, p. 187.

[33]

loyally the duties assigned to them by the Government of the day, of whatever political persuasion.

But this loyalty is subject to very varying interpretations – which can suddenly become critical to a civil servant who believes that the government is acting dishonestly. And the perception went through an important shift in the eighties. Lord Bancroft, the former Head of the Civil Service, explained that 'the Service belongs neither to politicians nor to officials, but to the Crown and to the nation'. But Bancroft was effectively retired by Mrs Thatcher; and Sir Robert Armstrong who succeeded him provided a bleaker interpretation: 'the Civil Service as such has no constitutional personality or responsibility separate from the duly elected Government of the day.' Much depends, as civil servants point out, on the accentuation of *of the day*. But Armstrong's appointment, as William Plowden describes it, 'implicitly de-emphasised the notion of the civil service as a profession – with a professional ethic of its own.'[2]

For most conventional civil servants the question of loyalty is theoretical. The day-to-day allegiance is to the Permanent Secretary, who represents the continuity of the Crown in the much more practical function of pay and promotion, and who is supposed to protect his staff against any unprofessional or dishonourable order from the minister. Ferdinand Mount likens the civil servants' relations with their minister to a ship's crew under orders of a pilot in tricky shallows: 'their duty is to carry out the instructions of the pilot, despite the fact that it is not he who employs, promotes or dismisses them and that his command is only a temporary one.'[3]

That is not how it looks to a civil servant who believes the pilot is mad or dishonest, and may stay on the bridge for many more years. And officials I have known have never been very confident of any check on ministers' powers. Few dare to blow the whistle on abuses, and those who do, like Clive Ponting, suffer the full wrath of government, which helps to scare others off. 'I have always had great doubts about the claim for the Civil Service as constitutional check,' wrote William Plowden in 1988:

---

[2] William Plowden: Whitehall and the Civil Service, from *Time for a New Constitutional Change*, edited by Richard Holme and Michael Elliott, Macmillan, London, 1988, p. 187. For arguments about loyalty, see Peter Hennessy: *Whitehall*, Fontana, London, 1990, pp. 344–6 and p. 368.

[3] Mount, *op. cit.*, p. 103.

'It reflects a complacency, indeed a naivety, about British institutions which history has all too often shown to be misplaced.'[4]

The civil servants' sense of profession has also been weakened by the changed attitude towards business, which becomes evident after they retire. As Sir Antony Part described it after moving into industry:

> The deification of private enterprise coupled with denigration – or an approval of denigration – of the Civil Service has had the effect of making it more acceptable for civil servants, not only in mid-career but on retirement, to move out into the private sector.'[5]

The change over thirty years has been striking. In the fifties most senior civil servants quietly ended their careers on retirement, and only very few went into business, with firm restrictions; particularly against joining industries which they had been regulating. But by the eighties most Permanent Secretaries expected to earn higher salaries after they retired, and were allowed to work for foreign as well as British companies. The stakes were raised when Lord Hunt, the ex-Secretary of the Cabinet, became chairman of the French bank BNP in 1980, as well as chairman of the Pru; and Sir Douglas Wass became chairman of Nomura International, controlled by powerful Japanese stockbrokers. Left-wing critics saw such transitions as a British version of corruption which allowed commercial interests to bring bureaucrats on to their side long before they retired; but it was really a movement towards the American system with a less professional Civil Service, with a less clear distinction between public and private employment. A few public servants emerge in retirement with independent views and alternative missions; like Sir Anthony Parsons, the former Ambassador to the United Nations, and Sir Arthur Hockaday from the Ministry of Defence, who both campaign for controlling arms sales. Some devote themselves to charities, or to life-long hobbies, like Sir Angus Fraser, the former head of Customs, an authority on gypsies. But most remain within the power-world which has enveloped their lives, reluctant to say or write anything which might rock any important boat: and eventually sounding very like the businessmen they were once supposed to confront.

---

[4] Plowden: *op. cit.*, p. 192.
[5] Part: *op. cit.*, p. 183.

Whatever the theoretical arguments, the real protectors of the civil servants' integrity are not codes but individuals: the Permanent Secretaries in each department, led by the Head of the Civil Service, who is usually also the Secretary to the Cabinet.

The strains of the job are legendary: Sir William Armstrong was so closely involved with Ted Heath's policies in 1974 that Vic Feather, the Secretary of the Trades Union Congress, called him 'deputy prime minister' (though Heath insisted that he never exceeded his functions as an official);[6] and Sir William had a nervous breakdown which was kept secret. His later namesake Sir Robert Armstrong, appointed by Mrs Thatcher, at first appeared detached and even sympathetic to the Social Democrats, but later became closely and publicly identified with her policies, testifying in Australia to suppress the book *Spycatcher*, giving evidence which he admitted was 'economical with the truth'. Sir Robert was well aware of the hazards of his job, as he showed in his judgment on Sir Horace Wilson, Chamberlain's adviser in the thirties who was the instrument of his appeasement of Hitler:

> It is arguable that to his misfortune and not primarily by his own fault he was thrust into a role at 10 Downing Street which ought never to have been allowed to take the form it did.[7]

Armstrong retired in 1988, to become Lord Armstrong and sit on many boards including Shell and Rothschilds; and he was succeeded by Sir Robin Butler, who looks the very model of the impartial civil servant, with the relaxed open-air style of a cricketer. He was appropriately trained as Private Secretary to both Wilson and Heath, and he remained aloof from Thatcherism. He reproved colleagues who became too publicly identified with the Conservatives and before the 1992 election he made a point of dining with Labour leaders and distancing himself from Downing Street. Now he works closely with William Waldegrave, the minister responsible for the Citizen's Charter and constitutional reform; but he also keeps a wary eye on Tory plans to privatise the Civil Service, to which his first loyalty belongs.

The face of the British mandarin still comes and goes like the Cheshire

---

[6] DNB 1971–1980, p. 19.
[7] *Ibid.*, p. 916.

Cat. Thirty years ago he was a shadowy presence scarcely mentioned in the media or parliament. In the sixties he emerged proudly into the daylight, and the Head of the Civil Service Sir William Armstrong waved the banner of reform on television. Later the television series *Yes, Minister* turned the Permanent Secretary into a lovable cynic who personified the reality-principle against the fantasies of politicians. In the eighties Margaret Thatcher appeared to confront the mandarins, but soon used them for her own ends, weakening their sense of profession. Now John Major promises a new era of openness: he has revealed the long-concealed details of the cabinet committees who conduct much of the real business; while Sir Robin Butler has welcomed the publication of a new *Whitehall Companion*, as a contribution to open government, 'to help you to find your way round the bureaucratic jungle and also to tell you something about the senior residents of it'. [8]

Yet the workings of the mandarins become still more elusive: for increasingly they operate not only within government but between governments. The British administration – 'Old Secrecy', as Bernard Crick calls it – still maintains its clandestine traditions: but its key decisions become still more difficult to follow, as they emerge from bargains and compromises made between Brussels and London, and reinforced by other traditions of secrecy from the Chancelleries of Europe.

MAJOR CIVIL SERVICE DEPARTMENTS AND POPULATIONS

	1991	*1981*
Defence	140,200	232,770
Social Security*	78,945	98,292
Inland Revenue	65,717	76,240
Employment	48,993	52,122
Home Office	44,097	35,482
Environment†	38,481	58,503
Customs	27,041	26,945
Trade & Industry	11,600	
Agriculture	9,737	13,218

* Health & Social Security in 1981.
† Includes Transport.

The main departments of state still have their own culture and rivalries

[8] Dod's Publishing and Research: *The Whitehall Companion*, London, September, 1992, p. vii.

with other departments, and their differences are fortified by their relationships abroad where they can forget they belong to the same government. The Maff, the Ministry of Agriculture, Fisheries and Food, has been the most Europeanised through the Common Agricultural Policy. But Michael Heseltine now wants to take the Board of Trade closer to the European industrial scene. And even the Home Office, the most insular department of all, is collaborating closely with other Europeans to trace criminals and immigrants. Their Trevi Committee is not named after the fountain in Rome, but after Terrorism, Revolution, Violence and Insurrection, the Committee of European Ministers of the Interior which is pressing for still greater official secrecy in their fight against terrorism.[9] Whitehall officials have come to enjoy duty-free excursions to Brussels, where they are still further away from their bugbear, the British public; and can be reassured by the grander bureaucratic tradition of the French, as they compare notes on the absurdities of politicians.

THE TREASURY

The Whitehall departments appear to have gained more autonomy from their old master, the Treasury; and in the eighties they were even allowed to control their own pay. 'The more complex, decentralised and diffused Whitehall becomes,' says Keith Middlemass, 'the more practical power tends to revert to Ministers.'[10] But Treasury officials still find it hard to keep their hands off the departments as they clamp down on public spending, and develop more sophisticated financial controls. And the gloomy Treasury building at the corner of Whitehall and Parliament Square, with its dingy corridors which seem designed to intimidate big spenders, is still more the central brain for the nation, dominating the political debate.

Thirty years ago most British crises and headlines were about colonial wars, global confrontations or ideological arguments: they were only secondarily about money, and few Tory ministers understood economics. Now even television headlines are about economic crises revolving round

[9] Shirley Williams: Britain in Europe, Thoughts on the Constitution, Sovereignty Lecture for Charter 88, London, June 15, 1992.

[10] Keith Middlemass, *Power, Competition and the State*, vol. 3, Macmillan, London, 1991, p. 424.

mysterious initials like the ERM, PSBR, M3, the IMF or the EBRD, which all ministers pretend to understand. It is part of the belated realisation that Britain is a commercial country which must pay its own way. But it has left a long time-lag in the understanding of ordinary people; and the workings of the Treasury are more incomprehensible than ever.

Within the building the armies advance and retreat in classic battles – between Chancellor and mandarins, between Chancellor and prime minister – but it is only years later that the details become public. When Sir Geoffrey Howe was Chancellor, Mrs Thatcher could briskly overrule him (for instance to reduce the top tax to 60 per cent), and found her ally in the Permanent Secretary, the tough Yorkshireman Sir Peter Middleton. Later Nigel Lawson established his own dominance over the mandarins – at some cost to the nation as the boom turned to recession – but they regained their control under John Major as Chancellor. The current Permanent Secretary, Sir Terry Burns, is a genial former academic from the London Business School, but he and his Treasury colleagues were united in the battle against inflation, and they effectively dominated the current Chancellor Norman Lamont, who lacks his own strong political base.

The Treasury is now much less challenged by other advisers. Thirty years ago governments on both sides looked for alternative economic opinions. In 1962 Macmillan established Neddy (the National Economic Development Organisation) as the instrument of national planning dedicated to high growth. In 1964 Harold Wilson established the Department of Economic Affairs, to counterbalance the Treasury's negativism: which reached a brief triumph with a National Plan, before it was dissolved in 1969. Neddy continued under Ted Heath, and even in castrated form under Mrs Thatcher, but it was finally abolished by John Major in 1992 – just thirty years old. It was little mourned, and Conservatives preferred to forget their earlier enthusiasm for planning; but its disappearance left the Treasury still more dominant, with its short-term horizons unchallenged. When a dissident think-tank, the Cambridge group run by a left-wing economist Wynne Godley, provided warnings in the late eighties that a continuing boom would be followed by a dangerous recession, their subsidy was withdrawn. And if the Treasury got it disastrously wrong, as it did then, the whole country from Land's End to John o'Groats had to follow its blunder. Only now do we hear from the former Chancellor Nigel Lawson that the Treasury forecasts were hopelessly wrong.

The Treasury has become less tolerant of dissent. In the early seventies, when it was committed to Keynesian expansion, it still saw itself as a kind of College of Ideas, and ministers could discuss alternative theories, including the monetarism which was being put forward by young Turks. But when Thatcher and Howe enforced monetarism in the eighties, against attacks from distinguished economists, the Treasury officials were pressed into a state of siege; and when Lawson was at odds with Thatcher they felt the need for solidarity. Today monetarism has been abandoned, but the Treasury is united under a single objective: reducing inflation. It is back in the negative role of thirty years ago, which made politicians determined to reform it.

It is a policy sensitised from human consequences: as eloquently described by the new Chief Economic Adviser, Alan Budd, who had explained his own worries in an earlier radio interview. He described a nightmare in which he realised that the fight against inflation – which he had long supported as a professor of economics – was undermining the workers and allowing capitalists to make high profits: and he recalled his experience of being isolated from his community:

Neighbours even drew the curtains when I went inside their house. They did not want to be seen with this rampant Thatcherite, who was associated with rising unemployment. I could see that the actual conduct of policy was causing immense strife.[11]

The Treasury mandarins become even more insulated as they are interlocked with financial experts from other western governments, preparing for summits, European councils or IMF meetings, all enclosed in their pure universe of money. The international financial mafia, Denis Healey complained after he was Chancellor in the seventies, was the 'last bastion of male chauvinism', and only comparable in its arrogance and isolation with the mafia of nuclear strategists in defence ministries.[12] Since then its scope has greatly increased. The collapse of Communism in the East, and the desperate need for capital from the West, have given the world financial bodies much greater authority – as if they were almost the reincarnation of the nineteenth-century imperial powers.

But the isolation of finance ministers and officials makes them unpre-

[11] BBC2, *Pandora's Box*, June 24, 1992.
[12] Denis Healey: *The Time of My Life*, Michael Joseph, London, 1989, pp. 413 and 417.

pared for sudden revolts of the populace; while through Europe they face blame for recession, unemployment and collapsing markets. As currencies are equalised and taxes are harmonised they all face the gap between the economic integration of Europe, and the lack of European political development and understanding. The Exchange Rate Mechanism inevitably became the political battleground. The Chancellor Norman Lamont used the Exchange Rate Mechanism as his support against inflation and his justification for high interest-rates, before he finally left it in September 1992; while his critic Sir Alan Walters explained that: 'the covert way to the super socialist state is a monetary union via the ERM. With one money in Brussels, power will be leached out of the old States of Europe and deposited in the laps of the Eurocrats.' But inside or outside the Exchange Rate Mechanism, British interest-rates depend on the policy of the German Bundesbank; and the only way to check the power of either the Eurocrats or the Bundesbank is to create an effective European parliament, which we do not yet have.

DEFENCE AND DIPLOMATS

Democratic oversight is becoming more urgent in two other areas of government which have become more internationalised: defence and diplomacy. The Ministry of Defence has been the most separate of departments behind its fortress in Whitehall, all the more segregated through its twin hierarchies of military and civilians, culminating in the Permanent Under-Secretary, Sir Christopher France, and the Chief of the Defence Staff, Field Marshal Sir Richard Vincent. The armed forces have maintained their status with the public while other professions like police or judges have lost it. After the Falklands War Mrs Thatcher gave new glory to the generals and admirals, particularly to her favourite the First Sea Lord, later Chief of Defence Staff, Sir John Fieldhouse. But behind the scenes it was the Permanent Secretaries, Sir Frank Cooper (now Lord Cooper) and Sir Michael Quinlan who were the real heroes, as they master-minded the strategy, first of the Falklands War, then of the British engagement in the Gulf War.

The armed forces have shown more flexibility than many civilian bureaucracies; and the Ministry has successfully tamed the three services to collaborate and adapt to world changes. 'When I first worked at the Ministry it used to be a small post-office between the three services, engaged in combat with each other,' said one senior civil servant: 'now there's a genuine single defence staff: there's still rivalry, but it's open, not poker-playing.' When I visited the Joint Services College at Greenwich – where senior officers are prepared for the political hazards at the top – I was surprised to find them more open-minded and questioning about the modern world than most businessmen; while modern air marshals or generals are less bloodthirsty – as the Gulf War reminded us – than many right-wing politicians.

All that flexibility will be needed; for the end of the Cold War calls for a drastic rethinking of Britain's defence, with a difficult 'time-scale mismatch'. All the British equipment in the Gulf War was conceived at least ten years earlier; and the first nuclear submarine HMS *Vanguard*, which went into service in 1992, was first approved fifteen years before. Now the collapse of Soviet power puts the whole nuclear strategy in doubt.

But the British public and politicians are slow to comprehend the change: they are less prepared to question a high defence budget than Americans or Europeans, and are still very proud of their forces which have nearly always won their wars. The British have no conscription, like the continentals, which removes their armed forces further from public view, and enhances their prestige. The Germans, who spend only 2 per cent of GNP on defence, have willingly abandoned their share in the European Fighter since the end of the Cold War led to bold 'Options for Change'; but the British have been more reluctant to cut their armed forces. Even defence officials are surprised by the public's willingness to pay heavily for defence when the threat to the islands has visibly receded – to the neglect of other investments, above all education. And only a few members of parliament care to point out the contrast, like the Tory George Walden:

> We are the poorest of the four largest countries of Europe, yet as a percentage of GNP we spend far more than anyone else on defence. We have a large and skilled army on the Rhine and an army of semi-literate unemployables at home. We have well-equipped forces to help us win wars which seem increasingly unlikely to happen, while we strive to win contracts with an under-skilled and under-educated workforce . . .[13]

[13] Speech to Chatham House, June 7, 1990.

But barring a global disaster, British forces are likely to be cut further, and to become more integrated with her allies: for despite the freak of the Falklands, Britain is unlikely to go to war again on her own. Service leaders have become increasingly part of a western network, linked through international committees, informal meetings and seminars, or country-house gatherings like Ditchley Park (director: Sir Michael Quinlan). They are developing into a powerful like-minded élite, but unlike the financial élite they are more Atlanticist than European: mostly 'Natonians' with a transatlantic perspective, strongly influenced by Washington, informed by American intelligence, and firmly rejecting the French vision of Europe without America.

Diplomats, unlike generals and admirals, have always been exposed to mockery and distrust from the public, as the first scapegoats for any international setback. The Foreign Secretary Douglas Hurd, a former diplomat, is well type-cast, always looking distressed by the public's ignorance and presumption. Diplomacy and democracy, as de Tocqueville observed in America, can never be reconciled, and while populists demand 'open agreements, openly arrived at', diplomats only thrive behind closed doors – making agreements which can then explode in their faces.

The Foreign Office is especially vulnerable because it is so closely identified with the European Community. It failed to realise its importance in the fifties, but now the 'Europeans' among the diplomats are more likely to reach the top, as Atlanticists or Arabists once were. Mrs Thatcher treated them as 'Eurofanatics' and effectively ran her own foreign policy from Number Ten, rewriting the speeches of her Foreign Secretary Sir Geoffrey Howe, with the help of her Private Secretary Charles Powell who shared many of her worries about Europe. She despised the European pressure towards consensus, as I discovered when I once interviewed her just after her Foreign Secretary Lord Carrington had made some concessions in Brussels: when I mentioned the word consensus she exploded, 'Consensus! Poof! What consensus was there between the early Christians and the Romans?'

When John Major took over he made peace with the Foreign Office and left Douglas Hurd to pursue a more European course. But the diplomats across Europe were too absorbed in their self-enclosed world, of intergovernmental committees, summits, receptions and mutual massage, to notice the misgivings of the wider public. The grand old palaces where they met may have encouraged illusions that they were back in the Concert of Powers before vulgar democracy interfered with high diplomacy.

They all scaled more rarefied heights in late 1991 when they began to negotiate the Treaty of Maastricht, which drastically amended and strengthened the Treaty of Rome to prepare for, among other things, a common currency and central bank. The British parliament debated it more fully than others, but the government took care not to publicise the Treaty itself: it was hard to find in any bookshop and cost £8, while in France it was on newsstands for fifteen francs. When the European governments met at Maastricht in December 1991 John Major stuck out against the consensus and successfully insisted on Britain's right to opt out from the final stage of monetary union and the social chapter, which he acclaimed as a British victory. But he was now committed to a Treaty which practically no one in Britain had read, which made much bolder steps towards European union than most people realised. Its second sentence referred to 'an ever closer union among the peoples of Europe, in which decisions are taken as closely as possible to the citizen'. But it offered no effective plans for democratic control.

Then the Danes held their referendum, in which the Treaty *was* carefully explained to them; and they voted against it. Not until then did the British people – and others around Europe – become seriously interested. Even committed Europeans were alarmed by the scope of the Treaty when they got round to reading it. 'We made a mistake,' one Tory minister told me, 'we should have explained it.' In the furore Douglas Hurd explained that politicians sometimes needed a kick in the pants; but the Foreign Office rightly got the biggest kick, for they had failed to notice how far away they had moved from public opinion.

Over the summer of 1992 the Treaty loomed closer to the British parliament which had to ratify it. A referendum in Ireland approved it, but the referendum in France in September was the crucial hurdle. Though Britain was President of the Community the government was glad to pass the buck to France: John Major announced that Britain would drop the Treaty if the French said no, and the British opponents of Maastricht hoped the French would kill it for them. The media suddenly became more interested in French politics than at any time since Britain joined the Community. As reporters and television teams interviewed angry farmers and right-wing protesters the campaign gave the Treaty a reality in France which it never had in Britain. But after the pound was devalued and withdrawn from the Exchange Rate Mechanism the British anyway became more sceptical about the Treaty; and when the French voters approved it by only a 2 per cent majority its future appeared still more shaky. The Treaty which had first been launched as a push towards a more popular European union had never reached out far beyond bureaucrats and bankers. And politicians across Europe were belatedly calling for the reconstruction of Europe on a more democratic basis.

EUROPE AND DEMOCRACY

Long before Maastricht the Community had been extending its bureaucratic power with no increase in its accountability to democratic representatives. When the President of the Commission, Jacques Delors, warned in 1988 that 80 per cent of the economic policy decisions would be taken at Community level in ten years' time, he was not boasting but warning: that unless parliaments caught up with decisions they would face a popular backlash. Mrs Thatcher vociferously blamed the bureaucracy of the Commission, the 'politburo' as she called it, which she wanted to reduce to a mere secretariat. In fact the originator of key decisions was not the Commission, but the Council of Ministers which represents the member-governments and gives instructions which the Commission then executes.

The Council operates behind closed doors, with no leaks or minutes, as obsessively secretive as the British government itself. The government's rhetoric against bureaucratic monsters conceals some humbug, for it suits them to have scapegoats for their own secret agreements: and in controversial areas of regulation, including the environment and monopolies, they can shift the burden to Brussels. Mrs Thatcher attacked the Commission most fiercely for just those vices which she was spreading through Britain – centralisation and unaccountability – which were compounded by consenting governments practising them abroad, out of sight of their people.

Yet the European system may be better equipped than the British to provide effective counters to bureaucratic power, and to ensure the stipulation at Maastricht that 'decisions are taken as closely as possible to the citizen'. And Europeans have already shown themselves more able to defend human rights in the critical area of the law.

5

The Law

In July 1992 the former judge Lord Scarman, aged eighty-one, delivered a lecture advocating a Bill of Rights to the all-party group Charter 88, which is dedicated to constitutional reform. The theme had preoccupied him for twenty years, since he investigated riots in Ulster in 1969, and saw how anti-terrorist laws could undermine justice. 'When times are abnormally alive with fear and prejudice,' he said afterwards, 'the common law is at a disadvantage: it cannot resist the will, however frightened and prejudiced it may be, of parliament.' Now he believed that a Bill of Rights was more urgent than ever: not just for terrorist trials, but as a brake on the powers of an overmighty government: 'a government above the reach of the law is the menace to be defeated.'[1]

The British separation of powers has been eroded since the Settlement of 1688 first established a balance between the Crown, the Commons and the Lords. The Crown diminished into a purely constitutional monarchy, and surrendered its executive power to parliament. The House of Lords was cut down by the Acts of 1911 and 1949 which made it subservient to the Commons. Now there is a single centre of power controlling the executive and legislature; and only the general election remains as the check on the power of the government – which becomes less certain as one party remains in power. Facing this concentration, Scarman argues, the individual must be protected by a written constitution with a Bill of Rights.

Scarman had said it many times before, and many lawyers in the audience had grown weary of arguing the same case. But the context of the argument was changing; for increasingly the British were looking towards a European court rather than their own courts to safeguard human rights. And British judges, whom the public had seen as protectors of the individual, had lost some of their credibility.

[1] Lord Scarman: Why Britain Needs a Written Constitution, Sovereignty Lecture for Charter 88, July 20, 1992.

Judges have always been less independent from politics than they appeared with their grand aloofness. They cannot be sacked except by both Houses of Parliament, and they still stay in special lodgings with their own butler and cook, as in Chaucer's time. But politically they are humbler than they appear: they accept the full sovereignty of parliament to pass laws which they can only interpret as 'junior partners'; and they have always been more interested in protecting property than individuals. Only in the last twenty years have some judges, led by Lord Denning, made bold judgments against bureaucratic abuses of power. Since then the process of 'judicial review' of government has become bolder and more frequent, to the point when in 1991 the Home Secretary Kenneth Baker was actually found guilty of contempt of court when he ordered the deportation of a Nigerian without sufficient cause. But most judges remain wary of criticising government and parliament, and are inclined to see themselves as defending the executive.

The judges are also, as Lord Scarman warned, influenced by political moods in times of crisis, particularly when a wave of terrorism provides demands for retribution. And since 1990 the public's confidence in judges has been seriously undermined by successive miscarriages of justice involving terrorism. In March 1991 the Birmingham Six, who had already spent sixteen years in prison for having planted a bomb in Birmingham, were found to have been wrongfully convicted; and this and other blunders set off a succession of attacks against the competence of judges. When the Lord Chief Justice, Lord Lane, refused to acknowledge the failure of the courts to administer the law, more than a hundred members of parliament called for his resignation, thus denying the whole principle of the separation of powers. But Lane nevertheless retired early at seventy-three, and the Lord Chancellor reduced the retiring age to seventy.

The new Lord Chief Justice, Lord Taylor, from a Jewish family in Newcastle, had already shown some interest in reform and freedom from convention: he had even been seen in the Temple in sneakers and anorak. After he was appointed he promised more openness and talked about the dangers of judges' insularity, which he admitted was bound to affect judgment, and asked them to be more 'user-friendly'. He even advocated an end to wearing wigs: 'it would be nice if we could catch up with the twentieth century before we enter the twenty-first.' But Lord Chiefs often lose their reforming energy, as they are ground down by overwork and understaffing and the inbuilt conservatism of the profession. 'The last four all began as reasonable, sane men,' one judge remarked, 'and ended up slightly dotty from the isolation and strain.'

The government have rightly looked outside the judiciary to try to restore confidence in the law; and John Major asked a superior sociologist-businessman, Lord Runciman, to chair a Commission on the Judicial System – which is now looking at a range of problems including long trials for serious frauds. But miscarriages of justice raise doubts about judges as well as procedures: particularly about how they are selected – from a circle whose narrowness amazes foreign lawyers. The Lord Chancellor appoints all of them, consulting with other judges in a self-perpetuating system, and until recently all of them have been chosen from the 7,000 practising barristers. A barrister after ten years may apply to 'take silk', to become a Queen's Counsel which earns him higher fees. Or he may be appointed as one of the circuit judges, and be called His Honour Judge Smith. Or a successful Queen's Counsel may be chosen for the High Court, with an automatic knighthood. From there he may become one of the senior judges in the Appeal Court where he becomes a Privy Councillor and (though not a peer) is called Lord Justice Smith, or Smith, LJ, or the Right Hon. Sir John Smith. At the top he may become one of the ten Law Lords, who are life peers earning £100,880 a year, and known as the Right Hon. Lord Smith. These were they in September 1992:

	Age	Background
Lord Keith of Kinkel	70	Edinburgh Academy; Oxford
Lord Templeman	72	Southall Grammar; Cambridge
Lord Griffiths	69	Charterhouse School; Cambridge
Lord Ackner	72	Highgate School; Cambridge
Lord Goff of Chieveley	66	Eton; Oxford
Lord Jauncey of Tullichettle	67	Radley; Oxford
Lord Lowry	73	Royal Belfast Institution; Cambridge
Lord Browne-Wilkinson	62	Lancing; Oxford
Lord Mugtill	61	Oundle School; Cambridge
Lord Slynn of Hadley	62	Goldsmiths' College; Cambridge

The Law Lords are still more segregated from the common herd: they even lunch together every day at a special table in the House of Lords. Their educational background – all from Oxbridge, half from public schools – has changed little over thirty years, though there is now no Law Lord from Winchester, the traditional judge-factory. And the more junior judges have similar educational backgrounds. This may not necessarily

[48]

influence their judgment: a self-made judge from a comprehensive can be reactionary and remote, an Etonian can be gregarious and progressive. What is more worrying is the secretive and limited choice, with no equivalent of the confirmation hearings for the Supreme Court in Washington, from a closed circle which can be much too protective. At least one current High Court judge is considered seriously unstable, if not mad, by his colleagues: but he cannot be fired.

High Court judgeships still attract many of the best legal brains. Successful barristers often complain that judges' salaries are impossibly low: in fact only three barristers over ten years have turned down the High Court, which provides more security, status and leisure than the bar. But it has become too easy to become one of the 470 circuit judges, some of whom are visibly inadequate; and the rise of litigation and crime has produced an acute shortage of judges, which has brought several septuagenarians back from retirement, defying the hopes of a younger bench, while successful solicitors have not yet shown much interest in becoming judges. In the meantime many judges themselves admit that they come from too narrow and insulated a group – which inevitably influences both judgments and sentencing.

Their most serious insulation is from the prisons to which they sentence people, whose conditions were forced into public view during the eighties by riots and by suicides which doubled since 1986 to a record of forty-eight during 1990. More has been revealed since 1987 when an unusually questioning judge, Stephen Tumim, was appointed Chief Inspector of Prisons and began asking what prisons were really for. He was appalled by what he found inside them, which he described in outspoken reports. He deplores the more punitive attitudes of the British compared to continentals – who also have fewer of their population in prison – and wants prisoners to be given training to prepare them for a more useful future life.

Punishment fails to deter, as history and our recidivist figures show. Satisfying public vengeance by imprisonment is an expensive indulgence at nearly £20,000 per annum per prisoner, particularly if it provides an inadequate shield for public protection.[2]

[2] Stephen Tumim: What are prisons for? Nicholas Bacon Lecture, 1991.

The gap between judges and prisons is widened by the classic British class division which puts prison governors in a junior category, outside any kind of establishment. Most have been promoted from the prison service, firmly controlled by the Home Office which prevented them speaking out. As long ago as 1966 Lord Mountbatten chaired a report which proposed that governors should be liberated from the civil servants – like admirals in the Admiralty. But the issue did not come to a head until the gruesome riots in Strangeways Prison in 1990 when the governor Brendan O'Friel was at loggerheads with the Home Office; and afterwards Lord Justice Woolf wrote a report which called for a 'substantial change in the attitude of headquarters', to enable the governors to govern. Woolf insisted that the Director-General of the Prison Service 'must be, and be seen to be, the visible operational head in day-to-day charge of the prison service'. O'Friel himself, now chairman of the Prison Governors' Association, publicly complained that the army, police and fire services were all run by people who could brief the public while governors had to remain silent.[3]

At last, after further bunglings from the Home Office, the prison service was allowed to become a separate agency in 1992, under its own head, Joseph Pilling, who had worked his way up the Home Office. But the governors still have much greater difficulty than the judges or politicians in making themselves heard.

When most people say 'the Law' they mean, not a judge, but a policeman; and during the eighties judges were sometimes hard to distinguish from super-policemen as they accepted police evidence too readily. The police are inevitably the most visible arm of government: 'the anvil on which society beats out the problems of political and social failure,' as Sir Robert Mark, the former Commissioner, described them. Relations with the police are everywhere a touchstone of true democracy; and the British have always taken pride in the reputation of the Bobbies, as they were called after Sir Robert Peel founded 'the new police' in 1829. Their power was deliberately limited by their decentralisation under Chief Constables, each responsible to local councils; and only the London police, 'the Met', came directly under the Home Secretary.

The old image of the local Bobby has now faded: the growth of organised crime and the mobility of criminals required a more centralised force

---

[3] Talk to the Core Conference, July 7, 1991.

to catch them while successive riots revealed bitter hatred for the police, particularly from black immigrants. The force became more centralised and politicised during the long confrontation with the miners in 1987, when anti-riot squads confronted strikers every day: the Left identified the police more closely with the government; while Chief Constables and police spokesmen appeared more openly Tory. In the sixties the British looked with indignation at the brutal French CRS who moved in military formations against protesters; now the French look with disapproval at the British riot police. Law and Order became still more of a rallying-cry for the Right, and spending on the police rose by 74 per cent in real terms over twelve years after 1979, with no sign of diminishing crime.

The most disturbing trend has been the eagerness of the police to concoct false evidence, and the willingness of judges to believe them, which makes a mockery of the principle that a man is innocent until proved guilty. The reasons are clear enough: atrocities enrage public opinion and the media, who demand police action; the police are pressed to make arrests, the judges are pressed to convict and give maximum sentences. The process suits everyone except the innocent convicted – and those who believe seriously in justice and human rights.

HUMAN RIGHTS

It is only since the Second World War that British judges have become seriously interested in human rights, much influenced by Lord Denning. Many politicians, including Lord Hailsham the former Lord Chancellor, have supported the idea of a Bill of Rights on the American pattern when in opposition, only to forget it in power. But Lord Scarman and other influential lawyers have consistently argued that only a written constitution can protect individuals from miscarriages of justice; as Scarman put it to me in 1982: 'no bevy of men, not even parliament, could always be trusted to safeguard human rights, and therefore there was a case for judicial protection.'

In the meantime Europe has begun to assert its influence. Since the British joined the European Community in 1973 the Treaty of Rome committed them to accept judgments from the European Court of Justice in Luxembourg, and two years later Lord Denning described how 'the Treaty is like an incoming tide. It flows into the estuaries and up the rivers. It cannot be held back.' The force of the tide still took some years to reveal itself: it was not until Spanish fishermen successfully overruled the British Merchant Shipping Act in 1990 as being contrary to European law that it became clear, as Sir Thomas Bingham put it, that 'a United Kingdom statute is no longer inviolable as it once was'. Gradually the European Court was becoming more like a Supreme Court, the ultimate arbiter.

But more significant is the development of the other European Court: the court in Strasbourg which interprets the Convention of Human Rights. This convention was signed by Britain and fourteen other European countries in 1950, before the Community was planned, and was much influenced by the British legal tradition. And it put its principles in writing like a Bill of Rights, including Article 10 which begins: 'everyone has the right to freedom of expression.'

The court of nine judges is amazingly slow moving: it usually takes over a year to produce a judgment, I was told in Strasbourg, and in its first decade it averaged only one judgment a year. It can only take cases after they have gone to the highest court in the home country – in Britain, the House of Lords. But its workload has risen rapidly, and it has become steadily more visible: it will soon move into a futuristic new structure near the European parliament in Strasbourg, to be called the Palais des Droits de l'Homme, which the Queen visited in May 1992. It has even become more visible in Britain, for the British law has been found breaking the terms of the European Convention more often than any other country which signed it. And British courts have been forced to accept its judgments, including a historic finding that a prison governor had no right to interfere with a prisoner's correspondence.

Many lawyers, including Lord Scarman, argue that this European Bill of Rights should provide the basis of a British written constitution: it is absurd, Scarman says, to have to make the monstrously expensive journey to Strasbourg to defend basic rights. And Sir Thomas Bingham (who in August 1992 was appointed Master of the Rolls, second to the Lord Chief Justice) has supported incorporating the European convention into British law. Lord Browne-Wilkinson, a Law Lord, argues that since the convention confers no more rights than the British common law, judges can absorb its principles into British law without any special Bill.[4]

In any case, Europe has already adopted a Bill of Rights which British

[4] The Infiltration of a Bill of Rights, 1992, p. 21.

courts will increasingly have to follow. While politicians fiercely defend the sovereignty of parliament, their citizens are already having to look outside Britain for the defence of their basic freedoms. And the meaning of sovereignty itself becomes more confused with the more uncertain role of the sovereign.

6

Monarchs and Estates

Traditionally three estates have lain at the heart of the British system, sharing responsibility for making laws: the Crown, the Lords and the Commons. The powers of the first two estates have been increasingly eroded by the third, and they no longer appear as any serious counterweight to either the House of Commons or the government. But both the Lords and the Crown have retained a residual influence which is now being further undermined.

The House of Lords, or the Lords Temporal, have never effectively reasserted their powers since 1911, when they were subdued by the Liberal government's threat to create five hundred new peers. In May 1991 they briefly revolted against the War Crimes Bill which the Commons had passed, allowing the trial of alleged Nazi war criminals; and they also threatened to vote against the Poll Tax, but soon came to heel. The Lords have become still more of an appendage to the Commons as all of Mrs Thatcher's many ex-cabinet ministers have been allowed peerages (with the odd exception of Sir John Nott): the old battles of Sir Geoffrey Howe and Nigel Lawson against Mrs Thatcher can now be replayed in slow-motion in this long political after-life.

The life peerages introduced by Macmillan in 1958 were meant to add more practical, non-political peers of genuine distinction, with varied interests and expertise. But the concept was soon debased by the prime ministers' needs to reward their friends. Harold Wilson added an element of farce with his 'Lavender List' including dubious cronies, and the six *Daily Mirror* peers: ('only Baring Brothers as a private institution has ever, before or since, so enriched the House of Lords,' wrote Lord Jenkins). Mrs Thatcher preferred to ennoble financiers who had given to party funds, or dons who had turned out to be 'one of us'. Most professions on which Britain's future depends, including teachers, computer engineers or even the police, are hardly represented in Lords' debates. Far from increas-

[1] Roy Jenkins: *Life at the Centre*, Macmillan, London, 1991, p. 253.

ing diversity, the life peerages have increased the highly centralised patronage powers of Number Ten.

Further reform of the Lords remains deadlocked. The Lord Chancellor believes that hereditary peers cannot be abolished without undermining the monarchy: rather oddly, since the monarchy seems to be undermining itself more rapidly. Labour has promised an elected chamber, but still feels its own need to reward party hacks. Liberal Democrats propose to turn the Lords into a Senate, partly selected by regional elections. But all parties find it convenient to use the Lords as an old folk's home, or playgroup (as Lord Annan calls it) for their friends. In the meantime the frequent thoughtful speeches from the Lords are inevitably overwhelmed by party pressures.

The House of Lords still includes the 'Lords Spiritual', the twenty-two bishops and two archbishops who represent the Church of England; but during the eighties their presence only served to humiliate them, as sitting ducks for Mrs Thatcher's unprecedented attacks against the Church. The personality of the then Archbishop of Canterbury, Robert Runcie, was in total contrast to the prime minister's: he had been a Guards officer and tank commander but his approach was gentle and pastoral. After the Falklands War he asked his congregation to mourn for Argentinian as well as British dead; and he infuriated Thatcher by his report 'Faith in the City' which criticised individualist thinking and urged more welfare spending. His archiepiscopate, says his biographer Adrian Hastings, had 'been more profoundly affected by a single prime minister than any before him'.

When George Carey was first proposed to succeed Runcie in Canterbury many churchmen assumed it was as a ruse to rally support behind the more obvious candidate, the Archbishop of York, John Habgood; but Mrs Thatcher was determined to defy the Church's preferences and enjoyed her own patronage. Archbishop Carey has joined in launching a new evangelical initiative to bring people back to the churches, and has made his own attacks on businessmen's greed and the neglect of communities; but he has lacked the intellectual and spiritual power to carry much political weight.

The clashes between Church and State have provided new arguments for disestablishing the Church of England, which is one of the few in the world which does not have to raise its own funds. The Church bureaucracy has lacked financial realism – as they showed in 1992 when they seriously mismanaged their own investments – and many think it would be invigorated by the need to pay its own way. The Church has made no moves to disestablish itself; but it now also faces a crisis in its relationship with the Crown. For the Queen is nominally the head of the Church of England, and 'defender of the faith', while she is also head of a family now notable for its high rate of divorce and unchurchlike activities.

Meanwhile the monarchy, the traditional First Estate, is now being systematically undermined by the Press, or Fourth Estate: so that its symbolic and ceremonial role in the constitution has come into headlong collision with the demand of the mass-market for scandal.

MONARCHY

In the summer of 1992 the Queen was spending her customary week in Edinburgh, as part of the unchanging ritual of bringing the monarchy to Scotland. The royal household moved into the seventeenth-century Palace of Holyrood on the edge of the old city, at the end of the Royal Mile, below the open hillside of Arthur's Seat. The Queen presided over the usual garden parties and receptions, in this make-believe setting: guests were escorted up the wide staircase flanked by constables in bright blue uniforms with funny hats, holding batons over their shoulders – who looked suspiciously like Edinburgh businessmen – and assembled in clusters in the Throne Room to await the Queen. Among them was a group from the Commonwealth – the kind of gathering she is known to enjoy – including Australians, Canadians, Asians and also a radical black editor from South Africa. He was puzzled to find himself in the line awaiting an unobtrusive small woman in blue: 'she looks quite an old lady.' He asked a courtier: 'What should I say to her?' Another guest explained, 'Just don't ask her any questions'; but the courtier assured him: 'She doesn't mind questions in a small group.' The Queen approached, was introduced, expressed her sympathy with the difficulties of a black editor, and passed on. In her wake all the guests beamed as if they had been blessed, remarking on the whiteness of her teeth, the brightness of her eyes, and wishing there was a camera. The black editor said: 'She's *not* an old lady.'

The ritual was all the more reassuring in a fragmented world, when the United Kingdom itself seemed less united, and the Queen seemed to sail above it. But nobody asked the question which was on all their minds, which had suddenly erupted in the Press a month before. Did the monarchy have a future when the heir to the throne was at odds with his wife, when over half the family was divorced, and when there was open talk of republicanism? The monarchy was enduring a worse public battering than when King Edward VIII abdicated in 1936 – which was a comparatively easy solution.

At Holyrood the courtiers were talking unusually candidly about some of their concerns: about the relentless siege by the world's media, the inexhaustible appetite for scandals, the over-extended family, and the impossibility of answering back. The monarch's constitutional role was quite separate from the family, they emphasised; the television programme about the Queen to commemorate her forty years' reign had deliberately excluded her family and concentrated on her well-trained professional role. And the Queen was now playing a still more important international role: she had just paid a state visit to France where President Mitterrand had rolled out the reddest of carpets, and cemented their friendship. The Queen on her side had made a speech in French, praising France's achievement in building Europe, and the French newspapers had given her far more publicity than the Princess of Wales. In the midst of European tensions the Queen had navigated above the turbulence; and the two Heads of State established their own understanding while the politicians argued below. And a month earlier at Strasbourg she had made a speech to the European parliament – to the fury of the anti-Europeans – quoting Lord Salisbury in 1888: 'We are part of the Community of Europe, and we must do our duty as such.'

As for the question of national sovereignty, a courtier explained, it doesn't worry the Queen at all: her family after all had long ago come to terms with losing their own political power. It sounded ironic, when politicians were again protesting about Britain losing her identity, which revolves round the Crown: the sovereign was not worried about sovereignty.

Walking away from Holyrood I reflected how little the rituals of monarchy had changed over the Queen's long reign, while parties and prime ministers had come and gone. The more extreme the swings of opinion and policies, the more unstable the rest of the world, the more reassuring is the image of an unchanging nation with a long time-span and sense of history. The court even in Scotland can still generate its own aura, protected from short-term political or commercial pressures, providing its own values as a counterweight to centralised political power.

Yet behind the rituals the monarchy has been turned inside out in a single decade. Ten years ago the wedding of Prince Charles, reasserting religious moral values, achieved a new peak of glamour and global publicity: I watched it at an early-morning breakfast party in Massachusetts, where adoring American matrons waved Union Jacks. Eight years earlier Princess Anne had married Mark Phillips, and five years later Prince Andrew married Sarah Ferguson, with almost equal publicity. Now all three marriages have failed, and the marriage vows sound ironic. The mystique has disintegrated into arguments about salaries, tax-concessions and bodyguards watching toe-sucking. The two sides of the perception of the monarchy – the constitutional role and the soap opera – have come into total conflict.

Mrs Thatcher played her part in weakening the mystique of the monarchy, as her own style became more regal and she even adopted the royal plural: 'We are a grandmother.' She had an uneasy relationship with the Queen, who was the same age: at the beginning she returned from her weekly chats at the Palace, her staff observed, in urgent need of a drink. The Queen has been consistently interested in the black Commonwealth and during the campaign against apartheid she went out of her way to be friendly with black South Africans like Archbishop Tutu which infuriated the Tory Right. While John Major's relationship with the Queen is much more relaxed, right-wing Conservatives still regard the Queen's Commonwealth links with suspicion.

But the monarchy's problems have been largely created by the royal family, and their dangerous relationship with publicity. The apparatus of royal events and rituals, from weddings and coronations to funerals, was built up in the Victorian era to strengthen the image of empire; and a century later, in the fifties and sixties, the ceremonials provided an ideal subject for television whose hushed commentators gave them a religious reverence at a time when other religious ceremonies were in retreat. But while the pomp was magnified the imperial purpose was disappearing, and television and journalism could quickly turn from adoration to destruction.

The extended family added to the danger. The Queen was unable to restrain the minor royalty, even when subsidised by the taxpayer, who were expected to settle on their country estates but who insisted on their share of publicity in London. The courtiers of rival royal households compete for attention and cultivate their protocol: overhearing two equerries arranging an appointment for their highnesses, I realised how even the smallest task can be turned into a ceremony. State banquets are stiff with minor royals, with equerries sitting next to serious diplomats, while state visits no longer get the publicity which was their original purpose: the President of Italy was furious that his visit was hardly mentioned by the media. An extended family is full of traps. Thirty years ago the Queen's Private Secretary Lord Adeane explained to me the hazards of the long reign ahead, like Queen Victoria's, when a fickle public could tire of an ageing monarch and a large family. Today courtiers talk more urgently about the problems of the QVS, the Queen Victoria Syndrome. The present Queen remains a model monarch, using publicity only for her constitutional role; but the rest of the family confuses monarchy with showbiz and soap opera, and generates still more public curiosity about its affairs, quarrels and separations, on the pattern of Hollywood.

The stars of the show inevitably face the hazards of showbiz. The Princess of Wales, like Marilyn Monroe, combines a photogenic beauty and naturalness in front of the cameras with a private insecurity and loneliness – to which the royal family appears as unsympathetic Hollywood moguls, even though it could cause a constitutional crisis. The Duchess of York has created her own image-crisis by equating royalty with crude publicity value. The transformation of the jolly chalet-girl into the magical Duchess provided a romantic sub-plot, and she appeared to humanise her awkward husband Prince Andrew; but her own affairs degenerated into farce.

The collapsed marriages belonged to a different universe to the televised royal weddings; and the semi-religious mystique had evaporated in the face of domestic misery. Walter Bagehot had said of the monarchy: 'Its mystery is its life. We must not let in daylight upon magic.' But the daylight has penetrated into secret corners and most of the mystery has vanished.

The religious rituals cannot now be replayed with any real credibility. It is true that the Church of England was built on a divorce, when Henry VIII broke with Rome in order to remarry; and many later monarchs lived semi-openly with mistresses and maltreated their Queens. But the Victorians developed the rituals of coronations, weddings and funerals to identify the royal family with public morality; and when King Edward VIII had to abdicate in order to marry a divorcee, the principle was maintained. The royal family in public was rigorously opposed to divorce, and three decades ago the royal enclosure at Ascot was still forbidden to any divorcee. Now that rule would disqualify most of the immediate royal family.

The monarch remains the head of the Church of England, and she still defends the faith on every coin with the letters FD. But the title looks odd with the heir to the throne in a marital deadlock, his sister divorced and his brother divorcing. It looks still odder to forbid future heirs from marrying Catholics, just when the monarchy and the country are coming closer to Europe. The Established Church which was founded on a divorce could be disestablished by another one.

The instability of the royal marriages may be linked to the lack of appropriate spouses. After the First World War reduced Europe's thrones, the royal children could no longer be expected to marry only into royalty, and George V allowed his son to marry a commoner, Elizabeth Bowes-Lyon, now the Queen Mother. She was always depicted as a model of graciousness, though others blame her for not understanding her family's problems. The Queen's own marriage to a royal Greek-German has survived. But her children's and her sister's commoner spouses failed to adapt to the rarefied and antiquated life-style of the palace. The royals themselves are left high-and-dry, curtseying to each other even in private, with a court of flatterers, hangers-on, soothsayers and rich layabouts to protect them from reality. And their failure to connect up with contemporary life now threatens the succession.

In this predicament the character of the monarch becomes still more important. The Queen has developed her style through intensive self-discipline: as she puts it, 'it's all a question of training.' Her femininity and unassertiveness have enabled her to gain the trust of foreign heads of government, without threatening them. Over four decades she has successfully re-formed the public idea of monarchy in her own image; but the immense Victorian apparatus, from glass coaches to palaces, remains largely intact, and has created illusions for the occupants as much as for the public. And the Queen's own success makes greater problems for her successor.

Prince Charles began his career as Prince of Wales very conscious of the limitations of his own role. When I interviewed him a year after his wedding he emphasised that he had little formal authority, as the junior member of the 'family firm', whose important decisions were all taken by his mother. He was torn between his desire for a private life, and the advice of his great-uncle Mountbatten, that 'in this business you can't afford to be a shrinking violet'. He worked out his own idea of monarchy: after studying anthropology at Cambridge he came to think that there was still a primitive element in the modern British attitude to kingship which could reveal unexpected yearnings among ordinary people. He was determined to find areas where he could play a controversial role without trespassing on politics, and found them in architecture, the environment and patronage, but he did not follow them through. Later he became more isolated, with an unhappy marriage and without close friends from school or elsewhere to advise him; and he lost much of his earlier openness and rapport with his people.

He was always very conscious of the fragility of the monarchy. He had closely studied the much-abused Hanoverians, with a special fondness for George III: and he had no illusions about future dangers. He was well aware, as he put it, that the cheering crowds could quickly turn to booing crowds. 'It can be a kind of elective institution,' he told me: 'after all, if people don't want it, they won't have it.'

REPUBLICANS

Do they want it, and will they have it? Republicanism is certainly now talked about openly, as it never was over the last thirty years, and the Queen's cost and tax-free status has become a public political issue. But republicans are not organised, and have not seriously proposed an alternative Head of State. A ceremonial President is almost inevitably a retired politician who can remain controversial and divisive, like Waldheim in Austria: if Britain had been a republic over the last thirty years, Lord Home or Lord Callaghan might have occupied Buckingham Palace, and Lady Thatcher would be a possible future President. The dangers of any president who is head of both state and government, like the French or American, have become more apparent since the television age: for an executive President can easily exploit the splendour of his office – as President Nixon showed in 1974, in the wake of Watergate. At that time I attended a press conference in the White House, when Nixon had already been caught lying; but he could still manipulate the news, and intimidate the fiercest investigators from questioning him about his lies. As the press conference ended an Irish-American journalist whispered to me: '*Now* you can see why I envy you your monarchy.'

The greatest service a monarchy can render to a democracy is to separate pomp from power. 'It is at any rate possible,' wrote George Orwell in 1944, 'that while this division of functions exists, a Hitler or a Stalin cannot come to power.' And this safeguard looked more important as the reign of Margaret Thatcher became increasingly autocratic. Even with a real queen in place, she had become alarmingly regal: without a queen she would have become terrifying.

The British are unlikely to abandon the advantages of a hereditary monarchy, which is part of their image of national identity – and other nations' picture of themselves. The continuous role of the Crown, which emerges from previous chapters, can only be associated with a dynasty, not with an elected President. The royal crest in the courts of justice, the crown on the civil servant's briefcase, the royal opening of parliament, the prime minister's weekly visit to the palace, all depend on the concept of the impartiality of the Crown: the American alternative of 'we, the people' still seems an ocean away.

There is nothing new about the gap between the grandeur of the Crown and the human failings of the royal family, which has weathered worse crises in the past. The monarchy still projects a long historical perspective that politicians have lost, which becomes rarer and more valuable as politics become more preoccupied with the short-term market place. And the royal family, with all their failings, can still attract greater awe among ordinary British people than film stars or other celebrities, which can be effectively mobilised, particularly for charities. Fund-raisers know that there is nothing like an HRH to attract big donors; and an arrogant tycoon can still be reduced to cringing obedience, as he bows low to a royal personage and writes out another large cheque for a charity.

'The monarchy has become our only truly popular institution,' wrote the Conservative interpreter of the constitution, Lord St John, in 1982, at the peak of the monarchy's appeal: 'at a time when the House of Commons has declined in public esteem and the Lords is a matter of controversy. The monarchy is, in a real sense, underpinning the other two estates of the realm.' A decade later, that judgment seems extravagant. But all the three powers – Crown, Lords and Commons – lost esteem in the eighties, and were diminished by the concentrated power of government.

The monarchy has often in the past shown its skill in survival and adaptation, with the help of private secretaries and advisers who shrewdly judged the political hazards. Now the advice has failed and the family hype works against the constitutional role. The obvious solution appears easy: to demote the family, cut back the civil list, royal flights, perks and banquets, while concentrating the pomp and privilege on the Queen. In practice it is not so easy; for it is after all a family, with its own loyalties, prejudices and priorities. And as the Queen approaches her seventies, the problem of inheritance looms larger.

Any successor will face a growing contradiction. The influence and constitutional role depend on retaining a façade which pretends that the royal family are different from ordinary people. Yet the media compete to destroy that façade, gaining quick extra circulation and profits by denying the family any privacy or dignity. The myth of the monarchy confronts the full power of unconstrained market forces – which it cannot withstand. A future monarch may simply find the job description impossible.

But the royal family have added their own obstacles to gaining their people's support in the next century. For their narrow old-fashioned life-style, revolving round stables, grouse-moors and large country-houses, has become more closely identified with the class-conscious pursuit of money and status. During and after the Second World War, the monarchy prided itself on being detached from the class arrogance of the aristocracy, and able to move naturally among all kinds of people. But in the eighties, with all the competitive advertising and social ambitions, the royal family became more obviously identified with wealth and privilege, and were helping to sustain the recurring British disease, of class.

7
Students

'As long as you maintain that damned class-ridden society of yours,' said Helmut Schmidt when he visited Britain as Chancellor of Germany, 'you will never get out of your mess.' It is a familiar charge which, like most British, I have got tired of hearing from foreigners who maintain their own kinds of class divisions. Yet national characters look clearer from outside than inside; and the British class system has always been like an onion revealing still deeper layers. Over thirty years British governments have been led by five successive prime ministers none of whom went to a fee-paying public school: today John Major who left school at sixteen can claim more plausibly than Thatcher or Heath to be a man of the people, and the prophet of a classless society. Yet the tribes at the top of the political heap have changed on a very limited front. Macmillan's cabinet dominated by Oxford Etonians gave way to Harold Wilson's Oxford dons, and then to Ted Heath's Oxford set. Mrs Thatcher fired Etonians and preferred Cambridge to Oxford, while John Major is still surrounded by Cambridge men. The more the old universities are opened up to comprehensives and day schools, the more they cultivate their privilege; while the political class itself becomes more distinct and cut off from voters in its Westminster hothouse.

The causes of the British class system go deep into history, but it has always been linked to an educational system which is in striking contrast with Europe's and Japan's, both at the top and the bottom.

At the bottom the British remain abysmally lacking in basic training for productive jobs. Among major industrialised countries Britain has proportionately the lowest numbers of sixteen- to eighteen-year-olds in full-time education and training: only 35 per cent in 1987, compared to 49 per cent in Germany and 69 per cent in France, 77 per cent in Japan and 80 per cent in the US.[1] In an age of electronics, computers and robots, the Japanese have shown that a well-educated workforce is the key to

[1] *Social Trends*, 1992, p. 60.

industrial success; while the British cannot produce enough trained people in critical areas, including computer technicians. 'It's the most terrifying thing about this country,' said David Sainsbury, now chairman of Sainsbury's, 'which puts us at a huge disadvantage in world markets in future.'

For those at school, standards showed little improvement during the prosperous eighties, and total spending on education went down from 5.6 per cent of the GDP to 5.0 per cent in a decade. Already in the late seventies ignorance at the level of the three R's was an open scandal; and the Labour prime minister James Callaghan called for a National Curriculum, to ensure minimum standards. But when the Conservatives came to power in 1979 they gave education a low priority. They were obsessed with privatising everyone, even inspectors of schools; and their competition theory was incompatible with the need to maintain basic standards for the whole population. It was not until the end of the Tory decade, with the lack of literacy and numeracy of school-leavers inescapable, that the 1988 Education Act eventually imposed a National Curriculum.

By then the teachers were in serious disarray. The Conservatives were keener to confront the big teachers' union than to improve morale. The teachers reacted with damaging strike action which played into the hands of the government, while further demoralising the schools. Teachers' pay fell back. In 1974 their average salary was 137 per cent of that of all non-manual workers; by 1992 it was estimated at 99 per cent. A teacher with four years' experience in 1991 was earning £14,260 compared to £16,300 for a civil engineer at a similar age, £19,800 for a solicitor, and £22,200 for an accountant in the finance sector.[2]

The decline of educational standards and resources aroused remarkably little interest amongst politicians, businessmen and other leaders, most of whom, or whose children, had been through a quite separate system. And it is the segregation of the old public schools, or 'independent schools', which most distinguishes England (not Scotland) from every other country in Europe. Middle-class parents in the eighties earned higher salaries and paid lower taxes: this produced a bonanza for the independent fee-paying schools, which went up from 5 per cent of the population in 1976 to 7 per cent in 1990: for pupils aged sixteen or over it went up from 13 per cent to 16 per cent.[3]

---

[2] National Union of Teachers: *An Investment for the Future*, 1992.
[3] *Social Trends*, 1992, p. 56.

The old public school élites, though they still crop up through this tour, are less dominant than thirty years ago in the British power structure. Even their Old Boy Nets, which provided so much mutual help in the past, are being rivalled by the more deliberate 'networking' of younger age-groups linked by common ambition. Eton can only muster two cabinet ministers, Hurd and Waldegrave: it still provides the Governor of the Bank of England and a clutch of City chairmen, but it is now more evident in the cultural establishment, producing the chairmen of Sotheby's and Christies (Lords Gowrie and Carrington), of Covent Garden (Angus Stirling) or of the National Gallery (where a Baring has succeeded a Rothschild, maintaining the old bankers' rivalry). Winchester can still claim two chairmen among the four big banks – Sir Jeremy Morse and Andrew Buxton – but it has retreated from its peak in the early eighties, when it produced the Home Secretary, the Chancellor and two Law Lords: now there is no Wykehamist in the cabinet, or among the Law Lords.

In academic terms many of the most expensive schools have fallen behind the cheaper day schools, the former grammar schools. When in March 1992 the *Financial Times* compiled a list of the most successful independent schools, based on results of all their sixth-form A-level candidates, the top three were all former grammar schools, while some more famous schools like Rugby (94) and Stowe (271) were right down the list. These were the top ten, with the predominant gender of the pupils (most now include some of the opposite gender, particularly in the sixth form):

1 King Edward's, Birmingham (boys)
2 King Edward VI High, Birmingham (girls)
3 Portsmouth High (girls)
4 Winchester College (boys)
5 King's School, Chester (boys)
6 Queen's School, Chester (girls)
7 Eton College, Windsor (boys)
8 St Paul's, London (boys)
9 Haberdashers' Aske's, Elstree (boys)
10 Westminster (boys)

The publicised academic league tables have themselves intensified the competition into a still narrower field. Nearly all head-teachers agree that other elements of a child's education are more important: the cleverest boys often later fizzle out, or lack understanding of people and politics;

while the less clever are more adaptable, and head boys and sportsmen are often more self-confident all-rounders than top scholars. But only exam results can be measured and listed, and as independent schools concentrate on these marks, at the cost of broader development, they intensify a rat race which the schools will find still harder to win.

For the recession and rising costs have now brought many of them into difficulties: their fees went up by about 12 per cent a year between 1990 and 1992, largely because of teachers' pay rises; while their pupils fell in 1991 by over a thousand, to 608,000. Some schools look towards state assistance; and in June 1992 the Independent Schools Information Service asked for them to be allowed to join the 'grant-maintained' system (see below), to become less dependent on rich parents. 'The whole trend is towards a mixed system,' said Father Milroy, the headmaster of Ampleforth and chairman of the Headmasters' Conference: 'public and private working together, and parents mixing as never before.'

STATE SCHOOLS

But this has been said before over the last thirty years; and the state system on which the other 93 per cent of the population depend is once again in upheaval. In the eighties some comprehensive schools showed signs of improvement as the total number of pupils had fallen, and schools had become smaller: out of nearly 4,000 comprehensive schools, 55 per cent had fewer than 800 pupils in 1990, compared to 36 per cent in 1980. Classes also became smaller: 91 per cent of classes in secondary schools had fewer than thirty-one pupils in 1990 compared to 84 per cent in 1977. The number of boys leaving school with at least one O-level had gone up from 49 per cent to 60 per cent in the thirteen years to 1989, and the number of girls by far more – from 52 per cent to 67 per cent.[4]

A few outstanding comprehensives in middle-class areas maintained very high standards and a steady flow into the best universities; but most state schools had lower expectations and inadequate funding. They were more neglected than the independent schools, partly because the most influential parents, including the politicians, did not use them. George Walden, a former Tory minister for higher education, has imagined how different it would be without independent schools: 'The breakfast tables

---

[4] *Social Trends*, 1992, pp. 55–7.

of Tory MPs like myself would be educational battlegrounds, as our wives described in lugubrious detail the shortcomings of state schools and insisted we do something about them.'

In the meantime the government has committed itself to a new division. The Education Act of 1988 enabled heads of state schools to 'opt out' from the control of local authorities and receive grants direct from the government. It was billed as giving more choice for parents; in fact it gives more choice for the schools to select the brightest pupils.

Forty years ago there was a surge of indignation against the notorious eleven-plus exam which seeded out the cleverest children into grammar schools. This led to successive Royal Commissions and reports about the division between 'eggheads and serfs'. In 1958 Michael Young (now Lord Young) wrote his book *The Rise of the Meritocracy* – a word he invented – which foresaw the emergence of a segregated, highly educated élite which denied all opportunities to the uneducated who finally in the year 2033 rose up in revolt. There was a broad consensus – broader than many Conservatives now like to remember – that such segregation would be intolerable.

By the sixties both parties were committed to establishing comprehensive schools and abolishing grammar schools. But most comprehensives, unable to select their pupils, could not compete with the independent schools or remaining grammar schools; and many were dealing with problems of disadvantaged children or immigrants speaking different languages.

Now the new 'grant-maintained' schools can already discreetly select the most promising children, by looking at their parents' occupations and education; and by 1995 the National Curriculum will provide assessments of children at the age of eleven. The grant-maintained schools are beginning to look like the old grammar schools, competing for top results and university entries, while the less fortunate comprehensives will resemble the earlier secondary modern schools whose pupils were seen to be condemned to failure. It is an ironic commentary on the claims to be producing a classless society. The wheel is coming full circle; and Young's nightmare of a segregated élite begins to look more plausible though the revolt seems a long way off.

John Major himself insists that parents must be free to choose their children's education. As he said in June 1992:

I was brought up among people who had little. Yet we were no different from the next man or woman. We had our own ideas, our own hopes, our own ambitions. Just because you have little money, it does not follow that you need little choice, that you are fit only to follow where others lead. People in those circumstances long to have choices . . .[5]

In practice the real choice will still be made by the grant-maintained school, which can choose its most promising pupils at the age of eleven and leave the rest for someone else. John Major himself, who was condemned to the 'C' stream at grammar school, could well have found himself doomed to failure. And the real need for most parents is not so much choice as quality and motivation, without the fear of their children being left behind. Every government faces a dilemma in its educational system: how to give fair opportunities for all while giving full scope to the brightest who can provide future leadership and skills. The British reformers of the sixties were too idealistic and romantic in not foreseeing the pitfalls of huge comprehensives, run by heavily-unionised teachers. Both Conservative and Labour theorists were extraordinarily unrealistic and uninterested in the critical questions of standards and motivation. But their ignorance and unconcern were exacerbated by the dominance of the independent schools whose long shadow still distorts the whole state system.

British state schooling has been further muddled by the uncertainty about decentralising. Education Ministers were always surprised when they took over the job to find how their powers were strictly limited by their exasperating 'partners', the local authorities who had been primarily responsible for running state schools. Local councillors, voted in by a small proportion of the electorate, had obvious shortcomings and political bias. But the alternative of highly-centralised government control is equally undesirable. The previous Conservative government claimed they were decentralising by giving all the state schools much more say in their own budgets. But the 1988 Education Act and the National Curriculum imposed overlapping examinations and bureaucratic rules which put huge new burdens on teachers, with a flood of booklets and folders prescribing every detail of the Curriculum and how to teach it. It was hardly rolling back the frontiers of government.

[5] Speech to Adam Smith Institute, June 17, 1992.

In March 1992 the new Minister of Education John Patten took over amidst much expectation and some alarm. He would clearly take state schools seriously: he had been an Oxford don, is now a conscientious member of parliament for Oxford, and his daughter went to a state school. He is also a Catholic convert, and just after his arrival he delivered a powerful sermon in the *Spectator* about the importance of the fear of eternal damnation: 'the loss of that fear has meant a critical motive has been lost to young people when they decided whether to try to be good citizens or to be criminals.'

Patten quickly set about preparing the most ambitious new White Paper since R. A. Butler's Education Act of 1944, which he published four months later, including an opening essay by himself. The paper was called 'Choice and Diversity', in keeping with Tory theory, and explained: 'parents know best the needs of their children – certainly better than educational theorists or administrators, better even than our mostly excellent teachers.'

Patten grappled more seriously than his predecessors with the declining standards. 'We intend to create a stable system of education that sets international levels of excellence. Other leading nations have high standards and a high degree of specialisation. We can match and outstrip them.' And he insisted on defining standards from the top: 'pupils need to be told when they are doing badly just as much as they need to be told when they are doing well.' His White Paper envisaged speeding up plans for grant-maintained schools, expecting 4,000 schools, including most secondary schools, to opt out in three years, and primary schools to follow – all to be financed by a new Funding Agency which would ensure adequate schools in each area. It allowed for specialist schools, in subjects like languages and music. It gave government new powers to rescue 'sink schools' by sending an Education Association to take them over, and it singled out a single local authority, Birmingham, as providing inadequate schools: while Birmingham is credited elsewhere (see page 66) with the top two independent schools.

The White Paper accepted at last the government's responsibility for educational standards. But in the process it took a leap towards far greater centralisation based on the Minister. And while the head-teachers of grant-maintained schools would run their own finances and staff, they would be subject to a massive new bureaucracy at the centre: including the Funding Agency, the National Curriculum Council, the new schools inspectorate and the Education Associations to rescue poor schools. The 25,000 British schools would become, like French schools in the past, firmly under the command of the Minister.

The power of the local education authorities, which had been established at the beginning of the century by the Tory Arthur Balfour, would now dwindle. But schools still desperately needed contact with their community and their region, to provide both a counterweight to the centre, and an understanding of educational needs – particularly of immigrant, underprivileged, displaced or disruptive pupils – which cannot be analysed at the centre. For supervising schools, like hospitals, prisons and many other local necessities, Britain desperately needs regional leadership which can provide judgments without political obsessions. It is just this which has been eroded by the confrontations with local councils in the eighties. The stabilising of the educational system is thus interlocked with constitutional reform.

UNIVERSITIES

The universities reflected social change faster and earlier than the schools, bringing them closer to a European pattern. British students have been among the most privileged in the world. Traditionally it was universities which were the social changing-rooms. Young people going to universities from modest backgrounds could live away from home for the first time, find new friends, confidence and horizons, adopt new accents and clothes: not just at Oxbridge but at many other universities which still provided a comfortable and gregarious life. Universities did not necessarily provide the keys to power. The academic atmosphere of argument, doubts and analysis has never encouraged decisive leadership or salesmanship: and many successful entrepreneurs, like Richard Branson, Sir James Goldsmith or Sir Nigel Broackes, never went to university. In the recession graduates face sharply rising unemployment. But degrees have become increasingly required by most professions, including accountants and engineers, who see them as the first step in the ladders of management.

British undergraduates have looked with some bewilderment at the giant continental degree factories: 50,000 students in one small town, commuting from home, surge into overcrowded lectures, and often drop out before graduating. The big French and German universities have bred radical revolts, like the great student revolt of 1968, not only because of their overcrowding, but because students are rebelling against their parents on whom they still depend. When the French student leader Cohn-Bendit came to the London School of Economics to preach his revolutionary doctrine he was met with phlegmatic scepticism. When I taught for two years at a French university just after the revolt I came up against the full romanticism and double lives of the rebels: after ferocious demonstrations and strikes, many of the most radical students drove home to their parents in Neuilly or Passy.

The British universities remained privileged while the Europeans expanded still further. The reforms of the sixties were designed not so much to produce mass-education, as to provide rivals to Oxford and Cambridge: elegant universities with their own quadrangles, high tables and students' lodgings, while other provincial universities like Bristol, Exeter or Southampton were up-graded. In the seventies the university population increased rapidly, with the help of the old Colleges of Advanced Technology which became universities. But in the early eighties, while Britain was booming, the university population increased very little.

Then in the mid eighties the policy dramatically changed; and in the five years to 1992 full-time students in Britain went up by 40 per cent, to nearly 700,000. The Conservative government encouraged universities to expand by straightforward financial incentives, providing funds according to numbers of students, and making universities bid against each other to offer the lowest cost per student place in each subject. Some of the more confident new universities, like Warwick, prefer not to expand, but most join in the contest. 'Money is attached to students,' as Professor Ted Wragg puts it, 'so institutions fall over each other to push up their numbers.' The crude equations of money may have been inevitable in such a headlong expansion; but they imply a sad distrust of the dons.

The model for cost-effectiveness was the Open University, the television correspondence college planned by Harold Wilson's government in the late sixties, and still flourishing: the achievement of which Wilson was rightly proudest. The socialist ideal became the Tories' convenience; for Margaret Thatcher realised that the Open University could provide graduates on the cheap, and in the eighties it showed that it could expand rapidly while maintaining standards. Between 1970 and 1990 its students went up from 14,000 to 47,000.

The university population was also increased by upgrading the polytechnics in 1992. They had hitherto been seen as second-class institutions, without the respect paid to the German *technischen Hochschulen*, with lower funds per student and, unlike universities, regularly supervised by inspectors. Now the division between polytechnics and universities has been abolished; they will all be controlled by the same Higher Education Funding Council. The polytechnics will gain prestige but the universities will be subject to inspection and closer auditing, and will have to compete with lower costs per student. 'We are embarked on a policy which is facile, crude, cheap and damaging,' said Professor Graham Zellick of Queen Mary College in London, 'and in which present standards will inexorably fall.' 'Degrees from British universities will cease to be respected,' said Professor Michael Dummett, the Oxford philosopher.

In this hectic expansion the ordinary British students are being treated more like continentals. But other European universities will still maintain a strong advantage in technical education, with longer courses for engineers and applied scientists. Many countries are planning a new wave of expansion to keep pace with the demands of the new industrial revolution. The French now expect to have 90 per cent of their population qualified for university by 1999 – a policy supported by all the main parties. The British may see the continental university towns as chaotic and exploited by the student hordes: even Heidelberg, the ancient centre of German philosophy, now has 30,000 students, many of them 'perpetual students' with wives and families. But German students are closer to the mainstream of their countries' development, grappling with a future where needs and qualifications are constantly changing.

The British still cannot decide what they want education for. In Victorian times they were able to devise formidable new institutions like Imperial College to provide for a new technological world; but in today's world, which is changing much faster, they seem unable to connect education to the needs of the country, or any vision of the future. Politicians and educationalists are still distracted from these urgent questions by the charms of the two medieval English universities, which like the independent schools, cast a shadow over the rest.

OXBRIDGE

The faster the majority of universities expand, the more they contrast with the two ancient cities which stand like enchanted islands in the midst of storms. They are subject to the same rigorous financial controls as the rest; but they still have their unique legacy of real estate, libraries and separate colleges, with charitable status, and a self-perpetuating fame. Like the American Ivy League they attract large endowments from patrons looking for immortality (or colleges for their children). With such protection they can resist the pressure towards the European model.

Both universities have become more democratic over two decades, and have deliberately recruited more students from comprehensive schools which now provide about half of Oxford's intake (though the ratio went down slightly in 1992). They have also become less dominant in many centres of power, including industry and finance. But like parliament or the monarchy, they are more publicised and romanticised as they begin to fade. Their dreaming spires and gothic pinnacles, their gilded youth and bibulous dons, provide the myths for television series, thrillers or tabloid headlines.

They still instil an articulate style and self-confidence which sets people up for verbalising careers including public relations, the media and politics. In the age of 'a classless Britain' the most obvious change at the top has been from Oxford to Cambridge, which educated nine of the present cabinet; and when John Major bid for the premiership in November 1990 his campaign was largely run by Cambridge men, including Norman Lamont, John Gummer and Michael Howard who had all been Presidents of the Cambridge Union in the course of two years. And many public figures hope for an eventual return to Oxbridge, as master of a college or honorary fellow.

Oxbridge graduates are less clearly qualified to grapple with contemporary problems than the rival élites, like the French from Sciences-Po and ENA, the Japanese from Tokyo University or the Americans from Harvard or MIT: each with their own kind of arrogance, but with more worldly justification. With all its homage from overseas, Oxbridge has failed to reciprocate: for instance by insisting on undergraduates having a second language. Oxford, despite its prestige in Japan (it educated both the emperor's sons), has been complacent in exploiting the special Japanese relationship.

The most internationalised British institution is the London School of Economics, in its crowded corner of central London contrasting with the spacious courts and quadrangles of Oxbridge. Professors from every continent queue up at the bar in its packed Senior Common Room. Founded in 1895 by the Fabian Sidney Webb it has become the model for other bodies including the Sciences-Po in Paris. Half its 4,500 students come from overseas, and among its alumni have been J. F. Kennedy, Pierre Trudeau and George Soros. It has produced four Nobel Prize winners in economics (Hayek, Hicks, Lewis and Meade), and educated a clutch of current industrialists – Lord Weinstock of GEC, Sir Allen Sheppard of Grand Metropolitan and Ian Hay Davison of Storehouse. Its current principal, John Ashworth, a biologist who operates skilfully on the frontiers of finance, tried and failed to move it to a more appropriate setting: the empty building of County Hall, staring across the River Thames at Parliament.

Whatever their apparent privilege all the dons feel themselves much less confident and autonomous than ten years ago. Foreign visitors may still see Oxbridge as a triumph of continuity in a dangerous and fast-changing world, but more frequent visitors notice that one monotonous topic now animates every high table: money. Most dons are beset by money-worries: writing proposals for grants, fund-raising for their college, or adding to their own incomes. No profession has broken more thoroughly the old British convention of not mentioning money.

Mrs Thatcher was notably uninterested in using 'wise men' to bring impartial wisdom to problems. Royal Commissions, which had included so many university figures, were virtually suspended, and with them went most of the 'Great and the Good' – the public figures assumed to be above the political fray. By 1986 there were 4,212 on the list of the G & G in the Cabinet Office (says Peter Hennessy) including 931 women;[6] but Mrs Thatcher preferred 'one of us' in key jobs in every sphere. The authoritative reports which provided milestones for public discussion over the post-war decades – particularly discussion of education – fizzled out in the eighties. Fifty years ago the Beveridge Report laid the basis for the Welfare State and sold 630,000 copies; today there is no comparable source of information or analysis. And John Patten's White Paper on education in 1992 owed nothing to the Great and the Good.

Both government and business have built up their own version of academia, in which a sales conference is a seminar, an office complex is a campus, a marketing plan is a dissertation. Businessmen invite dons to country-house conferences to add authority to their own assumptions

---

[6] See Peter Hennessy: *The Great and the Good*, Policy Studies Institute, 1986, p. 23.

and enthusiasms. In politics Conservatives create still more institutes and think-tanks to discuss policies and Tory philosophy in scholarly style, provided they fit in with the party line. But the traditional academia of disinterested scholarship, with all its scepticism and contradictions, has been marginalised. In the drastic process of centralisation and conformity of the eighties the universities lost their ability to provide counterweights. Civil servants and politicians visiting academia in search of new thinking are worried to find dons asking anxiously about *their* thinking. And their confidence will take a long time to rebuild.

8

Scientists and Engineers

The academics who were most demoralised were the scientists and the engineers who had once been regarded as essential to the nation's future, and who were accustomed to special grants and respect. They felt their loss of status and opportunity all the more bitterly under the first scientist prime minister, and not surprisingly Oxford scientists took the lead in refusing Mrs Thatcher an honorary doctorate. But how far were they demoted by party politics, how far by wider world trends?

Certainly their glory had dimmed: no scientific name today can compete in fame with Blackett, Penney, Zuckerman or Medawar in the sixties; except perhaps Stephen Hawking the astronomer. Britain's Nobel Prize winners in science have declined strikingly; six in the five years from 1974 to 1979, four from 1980 to 1985, and only one from 1986 to 1991. 'Recent years have seen a dramatic deterioration in the quality and depth of British science,' said Professor Paul Nurse and other scientists protesting against the Tories before the election; and they pointed to the renewed brain drain. In 1984 13 per cent of the members of the Royal Society lived in the United States; in 1991 20 per cent; in 1992 an estimated 30 per cent.[1]

The governments of the eighties were determined to subject science to the market place. They obliterated the traditional 'dual support' system which had grown up after the First World War, financing research councils and universities while leaving as much choice as possible to the scientists themselves. The government's funding of science had declined dramatically: down from 0.35 per cent to 0.28 per cent of the GNP in the decade from 1981 – which was not offset as the government had hoped by fast-growing contributions from private industry. Of the fourteen countries of the OECD only Britain showed a decline in total investment in non-defence research (as a percentage of GNP) in the eighties.[2]

---

[1] According to Anne Campbell, Labour MP for Cambridge, House of Commons, June 11, 1992.
[2] For figures and arguments, see The Times, March 23, 25 and 27, 1992.

By the mid eighties warnings were growing. In 1986 a group formed a Save British Science movement. The next year the House of Lords Select Committee reported that over five years the general state of science was worsening: 'the overall picture conveys an impression of turmoil and frustration.' It could not all be blamed on Thatcher. Much of the decline had deeper roots: Nobel Prizes, after all, take more than a decade to be earned. Already under the Labour government Shirley Williams (then Minister for Education and Science) had warned that 'the party is over for the scientists', and under Heath Lord Rothschild's think-tank had initiated a new 'customer contractor' system: government departments would only commission research for specific projects which had to be accounted for. Scientists were no longer trusted to identify promising areas.

Before the 1992 election all three parties had played down scientific research, and Labour was no longer committed to a separate Ministry of Science and Technology. The end of the Cold War gave a real opportunity to redeploy the thousands of scientists engaged in defence, which still accounts for nearly half of all government's spending on research. But the Ministry of Defence hung on to them, arguing that they must be prepared for any kind of future war, and no party would pledge any major redeployment; even the Liberal Democrats watered down their earlier promise to cut defence research and development by half. Little is revealed about this secret research army; while the Chief Scientific Adviser to the Ministry, Professor Ronald Oxburgh (an expert on the geology of the Eastern Alps) remains in the shadows.

The neglect of science by politicians and others is frequently blamed on the strict separation from the humanities which results from the early specialisation in schools – much earlier than on the continent. The British political culture remains based on the humanities, and even when scientists or engineers, like Margaret Thatcher or Nicholas Ridley, reach the top they do nothing to bridge the gap. John Major who left school at sixteen has done more to encourage scientists. He has created a new Office of Science and Technology (OST) under a cabinet minister William Waldegrave, and has given new hope to the Chief Scientific Adviser, the Scots botanist William Stewart, who is even talking about a National Plan for science. But the gap is still wide, and scientists wonder whether Waldegrave will give science any more priority than Lord Hailsham, an earlier brilliant classicist who became an unlikely Minister of Science thirty years ago. And funds for science are much harder to justify now than they would have been a decade ago.

There has been no surge of interest in civil research to take the place of research into defence. Across the world scientists have lost prestige, as the earlier excitements about space travel, nuclear energy or cancer cures have given way to disillusionment. The worries about the environment, Aids or other incurable diseases have encouraged anti-science, and Green campaigners often see scientists as enemies, across the world. But British scientists have faced more of a come-down than most, for they were in the forefront of world discovery over the past two centuries, and their achievements have rested on a measure of proud individualism and autonomy. By the seventies they certainly needed to be more accountable, but like many other professionals, including teachers and doctors, they complain they are now forced to become businessmen to the neglect of their vocation. They fear they can never regain the freedom which is essential to their inventiveness.

Engineers are still more demoralised about their effectiveness as the crucial link between invention and application. It is a monotonous British complaint, traceable back to the 1850s when Sir Lyon Playfair, the Victorian chemist who had helped organise the Great Exhibition, first warned that British engineering education was lagging behind the new German *technischen Hochschulen*. The early engineers, like Telford or Brunel, were essentially tradesmen on the make, brilliant innovators who discovered and developed daring new technologies; and the engineering institutes rose out of those roots, with no structure imposed from above. It was a classless tradition: highly-qualified engineers were prepared to do humble jobs, and they still have a lack of side and self-importance which makes them refreshing company. But they were unwilling to organise themselves and reach positions of power, and reluctant to form hierarchies.

On the continent engineers developed more deliberately, from a military officer class into a confident élite: in France the Ecole Polytechnique has provided broad-based engineers for top jobs in industry and administration, and German engineers regularly reach the top of the industrial tree. In the second half of the nineteenth century, says Professor Angus Buchanan of the Centre for the History of Technology at Bath, 'the theoretical competence of the continental engineer gave him an advantage in the new fields of "scientific engineering".'

The prestige of the great Victorian engineers faded: the word engineer came to be associated more with the 'grease monkey' in overalls. Their narrow education and political naivety limited their influence and ambitions in boardrooms or parliament, while their aesthetic limitations were visible in British cars or electronics compared to Italian or Japanese. Repeated attempts to reform always came up against the proudly separate engineers' institutions – the Civils, Mechanicals, Electricals and forty others – many at loggerheads with each other.

There was a new chance in 1977 when Sir Monty Finniston, an out-spoken Scots-Jewish metallurgist, was asked by the Labour government to head a committee to reform the engineering profession. Finniston was appalled (he told me) that 'in Germany or America engineers were regarded as right at the top, next door to doctors; but here we found that engineers were rated below male models'; and he described how engineers fell 'into a subordinate role like well-schooled butlers'. He warned that unless Britain advanced the engineering dimension, industrial decline was inevitable and proposed a new Engineering Authority as the chief engine for change, to organise education and qualifications and co-ordinate the institutes. But when the Conservatives returned to power, they failed to intervene; the institutes dug in and the reforms were forgotten. 'What I wanted was an engine for change,' Finniston lamented: 'instead we have got a shunter moving along disjointed lines.' The engineers are still a divided profession, with low pay and lack of status compared to the continent – in sharp contrast to their old rivals, the accountants. The word engineer still does not distinguish between a mechanic and an academic. In 1991 17,600 engineers qualified from polytechnics and universities compared to 3,600 doctors, 770 dentists and 245 Anglican vicars.

The loss of status was spelt out in 1991 by Christopher Lewinton, the chairman of Tube Investments, in a speech which he nearly called 'The Revenge of the Grease Monkey'. Society, he said, must change its attitudes to industry and engineers: 'Until you can make something and sell it, no wealth has been created.' He lamented that so many British inventions were never developed in Britain – including liquid crystal displays, electron microscopes, optical fibres and microwave ovens. 'The engineering of a product is all too often seen as an end in itself, rather than as a means to an end. The lack of commercial awareness among engineers means that ideas are rarely turned into money.' He advocated bringing together brains, technology and marketing under strong leadership of 'high octane' people. The profession must campaign to increase its status, as the accountants did in the seventies.

But the engineers still face the same deadlock as when Finniston reported in 1979. Instead of an Engineering Authority they set up a chartered Engineering Council in 1981 which is now chaired by Sir John Fairclough, a former Chief Scientific Adviser to the Cabinet Office. By 1991 he was determined to create an overarching body, to which the institutes would cede some of their power: a first step towards Finniston's 'cherished dream of a single voice for the profession'. But it was still a dream.

Will the 'grease monkey' ever get his revenge? There have been many setbacks in the face of bankers and accountants: in 1988 an accountant, David Lees, became head of the old engineering company GKN. There are still engineers at the head of some of the biggest companies, including British Gas (Robert Evans), British Steel (Sir Robert Scholey), Esso UK (Sir Archibald Forster), Tube Investments (Christopher Lewinton) and most of the power companies. In the BBC an accountant (Sir Michael Checkland) was succeeded as Director-General by an engineer (John Birt).

Some engineers see signs of a resurgence. Michael Hoffman, chief executive of Thames Water, believes that they reached bottom in the sixties, and are now being accepted by all levels of management. He argues that the revolution in information technology has produced a generation of engineers in software systems which let them into decision-making where they can use their assets. 'Think of our strengths: powers of observation, trained to interpret results, trained to predict outcomes, trained to provide solutions.'[3] Hoffman plays down the need for engineers to organise themselves. 'The quest for status is an issue that engineers cannot themselves improve,' he told me. 'Market demand will improve status.'

Having watched British scientists and engineers losing out to accountants, bankers and politicians over thirty years, with the special sympathy of a son of a scientist, I suspect their disadvantage lies deeper. The boom of the eighties widened the salary gap between engineers and financial operators, which encouraged many of the best engineering brains to become analysts, management consultants or marketeers. 'If we call ourselves management consultants,' said one leading engineer, 'we can double our fees.' Forty per cent of graduate engineers entering the technical side,

---

[3] Speech to Institution of Civil Engineers, March 26, 1992.

says Lewinton, leave within five years. This testifies not only to the low pay of British engineers but to the lack of respect and authority – as many find when they are employed by foreign companies who pay them much more and treat them with greater respect.

The contrast of status is most visible in Japan where the engineers who design bullet trains, electronics or cars are treated as national heroes – as were the Victorian engineers – like Ibuka who built up the Sony empire with his colleague Morita, and designed the Walkman. Morita has his own simple explanation for Britain's failure: 'We used to respect British goods,' he says, 'but Britain has lost respect for engineering skills and making things.'[4]

It is hard to resist the fundamental social explanation of the failures of British engineers: that they are victims of a class rift still running through the educational system, with a deep bias against practical skills; which in turn leads into a wider rift between politicians and administrators on one side, and engineers and technologists on the other. With all the attempts to reform it, the British engineering profession still has what Professor Buchanan calls 'a posture which resembles that of an inferiority complex. It is uncertain about its scope and its status; it is uneasy about its relations with society at large; and it senses that it is losing out in competition with other traditions of engineering formation.'[5]

It has been a recurring lament since the first industrial revolution, but it has become more urgent again since the new revolutions in electronics, computers and high-tech engineering which demand more respect for technical skills and closer collaboration between engineering and finance. And the cost of the rift is revealed in the lack of vision and planning for the future, compared to the bold projects of the continent.

CHANNEL TUNNEL

While the British were angrily debating their relationship with Europe in 1992, a weird landscape was being bulldozed behind the Kent coast in the south-east: a futuristic network of roads, bridges and railway lines which narrowed into two holes like nostrils in the hillside. The raw excavations and straight lines have a quite different geometry from the surrounding

[4] Akio Morita: *Made in Japan*, Fontana, London, 1987.
[5] R. A. Buchanan: The Engineering Profession, June 23, 1992.

Victorian towns and winding lanes; and the expected rush of traffic from the Channel Tunnel will eventually bypass the local economies, as passengers from the fast special trains race on to London and the north. But the psychological shock goes far deeper. The story of the Channel Tunnel provides a dramatisation of British contrasts with the continent: the lack of planning, the insecurities, the opposition to public investment, the contempt for engineers.

Political resistance went back over a century, when tunnelling was begun in 1881 and stopped the next year after military objections. It was proposed and rejected again in 1913 and 1924, and then abandoned for fifty years until in the early seventies it was again proposed by the Conservative prime minister Ted Heath. But when the Labour government came to power they soon scrapped it, while maintaining the Concorde – which shortened the Atlantic rather than the Channel.

Then in 1981 Mrs Thatcher, despite her suspicions of Europe, agreed with President Mitterrand to study the tunnel once again. Her main motivation was to show that private enterprise could achieve it unaided: 'it was always that that moved her to support the Tunnel,' said the later co-chairman Sir Alastair Morton, 'not any desire for a Fixed Link with the rest of Europe.' Three and a half years later the two governments invited promoters to submit their plans, and by January 1986 two consortia were chosen to bore the tunnel, with a diplomatic fanfare. The British company was chaired by the former Ambassador to Paris, Sir Nicholas Henderson.

When legislation went through parliament it specifically excluded public investment; and Mrs Thatcher's faith in the free market seemed justified. But by late 1986 the problem of raising capital was just beginning, and the Bank of England stepped in to find a more ruthless chairman. They found him in Alastair Morton, an ex-South African finance director of legendary abrasiveness who thrives on nightmares. He nevertheless established a remarkable friendship with his French co-chairman André Bénard, an ex-Shell director and Resistance hero with a quiet style and long experience of battling with contractors.

Morton raised capital with great difficulty, for this long-term project revealed the short-term thinking of British and American banks. Morton insisted that any large-scale British business must 'think European' with longer horizons than governments or investors. But the only bankers who planned for thirty years ahead were the Japanese. Fortunately the government in Tokyo had a strong interest in bringing Britain closer to the continent. When Morton went to Japan in September 1987 he was surprised to find Japanese bankers competing to be included; and eventually Japan supplied 30 per cent of the underwriting for the tunnel.

The next nightmare was the rail link. The French were now leading the continent into a network of fast trains, to reduce congestion on roads and in the air; and in October 1987 Bénard persuaded his old friend Jacques Chirac, then French prime minister, to approve a new route to Calais. The French engineers pressed ahead with little political resistance from the desolate north-west towns which welcomed faster links to Paris. It was only this French vision, both to devise high-speed trains and to revive the economy of northern France, which made the tunnel possible.

The British had the opposite problem, of an already rich and crowded south-east. The decaying railway line to London was pathetically inadequate, hardly faster than in the last century. But the prosperous constituencies objected to any new rail route, supported by a powerful road-and-ferry lobby headed by Lord Sterling of P & O, who had much Tory leverage. British Rail was hobbled by plans to privatise it, without an effective lobby and with no vision of international transport. While engineers on the continent were planning fast trains from Calais to Berlin, and projecting three tunnels under the Alps, each as long as the Channel Tunnel, the British were still arguing about how to get from Folkestone to London. The problem of the rail link had helped sabotage the previous tunnel scheme in the seventies. In the early eighties British Rail thought congestion would be relieved by fewer commuters. But by the late eighties the boom had generated a new wave of commuters, and the existing lines were more congested than ever.

The tunnel workers had converged on the Channel from earlier projects in Singapore, Hong Kong and Cairo, with their giant machines. But the consortium of builders were piling on their charges, which escalated with every change in specifications and threatened to stop work unless paid. It was a traditional battle of wits. The British contractors were tougher opponents than the French, who had a higher proportion of brain to brawn, and more skilled engineers. Morton found himself effectively chief engineer, and faced down the contractors with all his abrasiveness, while the arguments approached deadlock. At the Bank of England, Robin Leigh-Pemberton who had put Morton in planned to remove him.

Then rescue came from America: from the Bechtel company who

offered to lend their chief engineer John Neerhout. Morton seized the chance, the Bank of England relented and in February 1990 a team of American engineers came over to speed up the project, with Neerhout as chief engineer. In December the narrow service tunnels finally met under the Channel, and British and French workers shook hands.

The costs continued to mount, more capital had to be raised, the final opening was delayed, but by June 1991 the main tunnelling was finished. In France the high-speed train route was forging ahead, culminating in a huge business centre near Calais and a terminal four times as large as the British. At Folkestone the terminal was also taking shape on time, including tracks for the special trains which would glide through from Paris to London.

But then the vision of the future suddenly collapsed. The special trains, it turned out, would not be ready until 1995. Soon afterwards the government announced that the planned new rail route to London would be abandoned, and that a new eastern route would be surveyed – but would not be completed until the next century. In the meantime passengers would transfer from luxury fast trains from Paris, on to the old stopping trains to London.

Rattling back on the train from Folkestone after looking round the terminal, I realised that the local citizenry saw the delays and dithering as part of their democracy, but I wondered how far this drastic implant of international planning would quicken the responses of the British body politic. Fast trains full of foreigners emerging every few minutes from a tunnel in the hillside would certainly make the British more aware that they had joined Europe than anything over the past twenty years. But this great engineering feat had only been achieved through a combination of Japanese finance, French vision and American engineers.

9

City and Bankers

In July 1992 the Lord Mayor of London was giving lunch with time-honoured pomp to the President of Mexico, which Britain had helped to finance for nearly two centuries. The 350 guests waited in the great Tudor hall, under vast monuments to Wellington, Nelson and Chatham, until a row of heraldic trumpeters sounded a fanfare, and a fancy-dress procession of men in robes and comic hats entered the hall, welcomed with a slow handclap from guests, and culminating in the gold-robed Lord Mayor with flowing white hair, and the small bald shape of the Mexican President who looked even smaller on a huge gold throne. They all sat down for the banquet, wives sitting next to husbands in City fashion to prevent any hanky-panky, while the band played Gershwin and Bach.

Then toasts were drunk accompanied by both national anthems. The Lord Mayor Sir Brian Jenkins (who turned out to be an accountant, and author of *An Audit Approach to Computers*) explained that Britain was the third-biggest foreign investor in Mexico, and that 'London has not become a great financial centre by keeping closed doors to foreigners'. The President explained in Spanish that the British investment in Mexico was still 'not consistent with the size and dynamics of our economies'. The fanfares sounded again, and at 3.30 p.m. the guests departed to catch up with their work.

No other world financial centre could mount such a theatrical display of continuity: my neighbour, a Baring, reminded me that Barings Bank had first financed Mexico in the early nineteenth century. Now London was triumphantly reasserting its old global role. Yet it was Mexico's triumph. For only ten years ago, when I had last been in Mexico (which was presumably why I was invited) the Mexicans were about to default on their $100 billion debt, an act which precipitated a world banking crisis. Since then Mexico, with the help of President Salinas, had rescued itself from disaster, at great cost to many of its people, and had been seen as a model of realism and recovery for other countries, including Eastern Europe. But international banks, including two of the Big Four in London, had never fully recovered from their rash loans to Latin America, to which they had more recently added rasher loans to property companies and shady billionaires.

And the City of London was now in its own state of turmoil. That Monday morning the stock-market had fallen by 2.5 per cent, after a 5 per cent fall the previous Friday. Between the fanfares and speeches, the aldermen wondered aloud how far Britain's monetary policies should be linked to Germany, and the functionary opposite me was worried about Frankfurt becoming the site of the future European Central Bank. There was talk about the continuing recession, the burdens of debt or the repossessions of houses, which one alderman told me had just reached a record. 'We could learn a thing or two from Mexico,' said my City neighbour. In truth Mexico had faced up to its moment of truth as a borrower ten years ago, more effectively than Britain as a lender. The London banks should have learnt a lesson from those dangerous loans which they had never properly supervised. Instead they had embarked on another lending binge at home, the full cost of which is now emerging.

THE CITY TRANSFORMED

In the early eighties the Thatcher government was determined to dismantle the socialist corporate state and to liberate finance and industry from controls. Tory as well as Labour governments had maintained a machinery of planning under Neddy, while bankers and businessmen were constrained by regulation, exchange controls and high taxation. But in the eighties planning was abandoned, exchange controls were lifted and the Big Bang deregulated the City, allowing stockbrokers to merge with banks including foreigners. In five years the value of the London stock-market tripled while the highest income-tax rates came down to 60 per cent, then 40 per cent. The liberation was not just national but global. The opening-up of markets allowed billions to rush round the world every day. But the British change of mood, after years of controls, was the most extreme in Western Europe: and in the excitement of freedom after fifty years of constraint the need for regulation and surveillance was brushed aside.

Over ten years the City of London had been transformed, and its spectacular skyline proclaims it as the financial capital of Europe. Its longitude, language, fast dealing and freedom from controls attracted

Americans and Japanese as well as Europeans; and the inrush of money spilt far beyond the 'square mile', into Docklands and the West End.

The British were reasserting their traditional métier as world traders sensitive to every distant market. It seemed like a return to the freedom and internationalism of the Edwardian world before it broke apart seventy years ago. 'What an extraordinary episode in the economic progress of man that age was which came to an end in August 1914,' Maynard Keynes had written in 1919, describing how a Londoner could enjoy the products of the whole world, could invest in municipalities across the continents, and could travel anywhere with a few coins and no passport. That world had been obliterated by two world wars. But now London saw itself back in the centre of a reopened world stage.

London is a bigger *international* financial centre, with more foreign banks, than its rivals New York and Tokyo (though they both deal with far larger domestic finance). It had 680,000 people working in business and finance in 1989, 100,000 more than New York. Its greatest revenues came from foreign exchange (over £3 billion in 1991) followed by international bank lending and international insurance – mainly through Lloyd's.[1] London maintains its lead over continental centres, but this becomes less certain as the European Community progresses. A European Central Bank, if it happens, will almost certainly be centred in Bonn, bringing much extra business to Frankfurt; and European dealers and traders are becoming more flexible, less regulated to compete with London – whose freedom from regulation in the eighties produced some dangerous excesses. But so far London has gained most from the global markets. As faith in Communism and socialism collapsed, the values of capitalism triumphed. Bankers and financiers could again move across the world to lend, restructure and reorganise countries on their own terms, with the rules enforced by international institutions in place of imperial armies and administrators.

More prosperous Britons were going back to the lost world of rentiers dependent on dividends and unearned income: the 'coupon-clippers' as Lenin called them, but now including a broader slice of the population. In 1981 only one in thirteen of the British were shareholders in any company; by 1990 it was a quarter. It was a misleading increase, for half

[1] For figures, see City Research Project Interim Report, July 1992. Corporation of London, London EC2.

the shareholders held shares in only one company after the succession of mass-privatisations; but there was certainly an overall increase in unearned income. Between the same years the proportion of Britain's household income from rent, dividends, interest, private pensions or annuities had gone up from 13 per cent to 18 per cent.[2] Conspicuous spending was back in favour, and shopping could become an end in itself, as in the Belle Epoque. The old Edwardian carriage trade shops like Harrods or Fortnum's enjoyed a new boom as purveyors of elegant life-styles, while the passwords of old-fashioned leisure, like Dunhill, Burberry or Cartier, were updated for a world of mass-marketing.

The transformation provided new heroes. Financiers and entrepreneurs had been out of fashion since the thirties. The archetypal money-men in the post-war decades, like Charles Clore or Isaac Wolfson in the fifties, Arnold Weinstock or Siegmund Warburg in the sixties, were in the shadows like owls. But the new breed were more like eagles or lions, and publicised like film stars. They were both rich and glamorous, appearing on television and writing memoirs: for their fame was good for their share-price.

The City, always a kind of offshore island within Britain, was still more cut-off from the sleepier mainland. But now it was competing with other offshore islands like Manhattan or even the Cayman Islands to provide freedom and secrecy to attract international finance without being asked questions. It was a young people's world, for global dealing and hustling need stamina and optimism. Older bankers who remembered earlier crashes deplored the hype, the rash loans and the short horizons. But they would not rein back the young dealers and salesmen who were pushing up profits. Few could resist the euphoria. Corporate memories were short and the money-explosion of the eighties was unprecedented, anywhere.

The excitement was most obvious in the talk about money. Since the excesses of Edwardian plutocrats, the British had been proud of avoiding the subject, unlike foreigners. 'The Americans always talk about dollars,' as Nancy Mitford had explained: 'the British never talk about pounds.' Of course this discretion concealed humbug and exploitation – doctors or lawyers could more easily sting clients who dared not ask about fees beforehand – but the taboo also helped to dignify those without money. In the fifties most salaries were secret, except for civil servants' which were

---

[2] Government Statistical Service: *Social Trends*, 1992, p. 90.

published every year in *Whitaker's Almanack*; and high taxes made them less relevant anyway.

The ambitions of the eighties broke through the taboo, and connected status much more closely with well-publicised earnings. Money-mania spread from the City into industry and some professions. Doctors and barristers made known their incomes, while schoolteachers were made to feel still poorer. Newspapers began compiling 'rich lists' of the wealthiest people: in 1992 the *Sunday Times* found 300 families each owning more than £23 million.

'The rough and vulgar structure of English commerce is the secret of its life,' wrote Walter Bagehot in Lombard Street in 1888, 'for it contains "the propensity of variation" which, in the social as in the animal kingdom, is the principle of progress'; and he praised the enterprise of self-made men who did not have the protective instincts of the rich. A century after Bagehot the conspicuous spending and self-publicising of the eighties proclaimed a resurgence of vulgarity. Sir James Goldsmith, who belonged both to the old rich and the new rich, insisted that it was a sign of vigorous change. 'If we only want people who have had a hundred years to learn to use money, to have money, we are clearly precluding change,' he told me in October 1988. 'So if we want change, if we want vigour, we are going to have vulgarity. It is one of the things which irritates, but is necessary.'

But how thoroughly did this money-consciousness change the basic British power-structure, or improve the industrial prospects on which most jobs depended? And how did the new corporate and individual wealth increase the cultural diversity, or the 'propensity of variation', and influence older British values?

The City was certainly internationalised by the Big Bang which opened the doors to outsiders, who quickly overwhelmed the traditional stockbrokers in their mahogany boardrooms. Their partners were glad to sell out to foreign banks desperate to buy into the market place: they made a few millions but often lost their jobs, adding to the numbers of bored millionaires. In the fall-out from the Big Bang many small investors were miserably neglected. Citibank, the biggest American bank, bought two old stockbrokers, Vickers da Costa and Scrimgeours, to provide a London base, and renovated the old Billingsgate fishmarket to provide a dealing-room. But after huge losses they pulled out, leaving an empty Billingsgate and thousands of furious small investors in the lurch. There were too many foreign banks now chasing too little business and piling up losses. Perhaps not surprisingly, the one stockbroker which remained independent was the most successful. Cazenove's, the blue-blooded firm founded by Philip Cazenove in 1823, resisted all bids and retained much of their business as brokers to the Establishment, as they used their contacts to place new issues with corporate investors. They increased their market share and made profits while others were losing. In the new world of global operators the traditional Old Boy Net still played its role, in shifting large blocks of shares. But the individual small investor played much less of a part: over thirty years the holdings of individual shareholders, despite their growing numbers, had been going down by over 1 per cent a year, down from 70 per cent to 20 per cent of the total value of shares.[3]

MERCHANT BANKERS

The traditional leaders of City enterprise had been the merchant banks, run by members of rich families with direct responsibility, who since the eighteenth century had been buying, selling and underwriting across the world, manoeuvring between big organisations like taxis between buses. They were nearly all Jewish, with the striking exception of Barings who came from north Germany in 1717 and established a distinct Protestant tradition. The bankers maintained their international links through the bleak years after the Second World War; and the freedom of the eighties gave them new opportunities, particularly in privatising nationalised industries. But the Big Bang brought stiffer competition with the international investment banks, led by Salomon Brothers and Goldman Sachs. A few British merchant banks remained independent, including the old rivals Barings and Rothschilds: their chairmen, Peter Baring and Evelyn de Rothschild earned £511,000 and £852,000 respectively in 1991. But many lost their autonomy, including Morgan Grenfell which became part of the Deutsche Bank.

The shining exception was Warburg's which had been set up in 1946 by a German refugee from an old banking family which could be traced back to a seventeenth-century Jewish money-changer in Pisa, Andrea del Banco. Siegmund Warburg was a pioneer who deeply distrusted the bureaucracies of big banks and in the late seventies he complained to me

---

[3] See *Deeper Share Ownership*, Paper No. 12, Social Market Foundation, June 1992.

that his own bank was getting too big. He died in 1982, just before the Big Bang, but his successors were determined to compete with the American giants. They were much the most successful British merchant bank, with highly-paid experts on privatising, raiding and corporate finance, and a team of advisers to Third World and East European countries. Their staff went up from 700 to 6,000 in a few years, and in 1992 their chairman Sir David Scholey earned over a million pounds. They developed elaborate management systems but still recruited staff with due attention to Siegmund's reliance on graphology. But Warburg's is now less cosmopolitan, and much still depends on the two octogenarian Jewish financiers, Henry Grunfeld and Lord Roll, Warburg's associates who could open all the doors.

The individual enterprise and responsibility of the surviving merchant banks was in growing contrast to the managers of the impersonal giant banks around the world, as they lent too rashly and passed the buck to each other; and the boom of the eighties showed up all the irresponsibility of gigantism in banks.

THE BANK OF ENGLAND

In the centre of the City, behind its windowless façade, the Bank of England is the ultimate protector of the depositor and investor, but its responsibility has become much less clear. Traditionally the Governor of the Bank was the City's headmaster, whose frown could terrify grown men and whose handshake could launch a career: when banks were crashing in 1974 the Governor Gordon Richardson summoned the heads of the Big Four and compelled them to launch a 'lifeboat' to rescue the victims. The inrush of foreign banks in the eighties and the new banking laws diminished the Governor's presence: after two years in London the head of the huge American group Merrill Lynch had not even seen him, let alone his frown.

In economic policy the Bank is now subservient to the Treasury. It cannot defy the government in fixing interest-rates as the Bundesbank does or as a future European Central Bank would be able to do; and the Governor cannot openly contradict the Chancellor. But the Bank of England still discreetly plays a greater role in the British establishment than meets the eye, quietly putting key men in key places: asking Ian Hay Davison to try to clean up Lloyd's, or Sir Alastair Morton to fix the

Channel Tunnel. It was much less decisive in supervising the banks which are the safeguards for depositors' money. It was the Governor's job both to publicly maintain public confidence in the banks and privately to make sure that they were properly run – like a swan, serene above the surface and energetic below. Robin Leigh-Pemberton whom Thatcher made Governor in 1982 was well able to generate calm confidence; but colleagues were worried by his inexperience in world banking; and the City's hospitality to foreigners had made supervision much harder. By the late eighties many experts on Middle East banks were puzzled by the continuing presence of a dubious bank called BCCI which had been refused a licence in New York, and even in Jeddah, because it was not properly supervised. But there was also irresponsibility among bankers much closer to home.

HIGH STREET BANKERS

The most visible new freedom was in the big banks in the high streets, the clearing banks or 'clearers' who can use funds from their millions of small depositors. In earlier decades they scarcely competed at all, with their old-fashioned hierarchies and strict controls on credit: 'It was like driving a very powerful car at twenty miles an hour,' Lord Franks told me when he was chairman of Lloyds. When the government relaxed credit controls in the seventies they competed more, not so much in services to small customers as in lending to big companies, particularly to property companies. They should have learnt their lesson in 1974, when the property bubble burst, and the Bank of England had to rescue fringe banks and one clearing bank, NatWest, came close to collapse. But by the mid eighties the new property boom sent them on another lending spree. It was quite remarkable, said the former Chancellor Nigel Lawson (rather too late), that they 'went on lending at a quite rapid rate, without I think recognising the risks they were incurring themselves'.

The banks were now competing for depositors with the building societies, which had begun (like insurance companies) as self-help clubs but were now major repositories of savings. The biggest, Abbey National, has become a public company, in effect the fifth biggest bank: the others remain mutual societies owned by their members, who had little chance to interfere with the directors. In 1991, as the recession deepened and profits fell, all their chief executives were awarded big pay rises: Geoff

Lister, the chief of the Bradford & Bingley, went up 48.9 per cent to £189,356.

But the real competition for the traditional banks was in adventurous lending, including loans to flashy but shady billionaires. The more secretive their client, the more the big banks competed to lend – whether to the Australian showman Alan Bond or the fraudster Robert Maxwell. The bankers' irresponsibility is hard to forgive. But when the media protest they reply that if you discredit the banks you threaten the delicate balance on which the capitalist system depends. By the nineties all four big banks were suffering from bad debts – from Third World countries, bankrupted small businessmen and empty skyscrapers. By 1992 Lloyds had lent 165 per cent of its equity to property and construction companies, Barclays had lent 148 per cent, the Midland 119 per cent: only NatWest, after its earlier trauma, were noticeably more cautious with only 87 per cent.[4]

In the late eighties Barclays and NatWest were competing for top place, raising the stakes in lending. Their staider branch managers were appalled by the young marketing whiz-kids who were encouraging young people to borrow – particularly when they lured their own children into debt. As the banks' loans deteriorated, many managers in both banks hoped that the Bank of England would intervene to stop their reckless contest; but the headmaster was not to be seen – until almost too late. At last after a major problem at NatWest the Governor moved, replacing the chairman Lord Boardman with Lord Alexander, a towering barrister aloof from the City. Barclays' chairman John Quinton seemed more secure: he was the first chairman who did not come from one of Barclays' founding families. But the Barclays board became worried about their risky loans and declining profits, and Quinton too was eased out – this time, to the Bank of England's surprise, to be replaced by Andrew Buxton who came from Winchester, Oxford – and an old Quaker family. ('It has always been relatively easy,' as its official history candidly explains, 'for a scion of the old Quaker families to reach a high position in Barclays.') Only Lloyds still kept the same chairman: Sir Jeremy Morse, the high priest of the banking system; and soon even he was to lose face.

It was the Midland which was most at risk. Its serious problems went back to the seventies when it bought the Californian Crocker Bank in a

[4] *Financial Times*, April 3, 1992

much acclaimed deal which actually brought a can of worms – a mass of loans to Latin American countries which became more and more dangerous with the debt crisis. In 1987 the Governor intervened, to put in as chairman of Midland his own former deputy, Sir Kit McMahon, an Australian ex-don. But two years later the Midland was still in trouble, without enough capital to compete internationally, and with high domestic debts. The Bank of England moved again, removing McMahon, and installed Sir Peter Walters, an oilman from BP. 'Recession had taught us the dangers of short-term funding,' Walters explained, 'and for this the banks must share in the blame.' Predators began hovering over the Midland. At Lloyds Morse and his chief executive Brian Pitman planned to bid for it, to the dismay of the Bank of England, now powerless to intervene. This set off a bid from William Purves of the Hong Kong Bank, which wanted a British base to balance its tricky future with mainland China. A classic battle ensued: Morse tried to argue that his bid would actually increase competition, but the merger between two of the Big Four would cause problems with the Monopolies Commission. The Hong Kong Bank upped its bid and won the day, bringing a breath of Asian air into the high streets.

The over-lending by the high-street banks had done more than put their own safety at risk. Their wild marketing of loans to students, home-owners and debtaholics had led to countless personal tragedies as interest-rates went up and the economy turned down. In the long hangover, customers who had been over-keen to borrow became over-keen to save; and the optimism of the eighties gave way to a pessimism which could be more dangerous, as people lost confidence in credit and preferred to avoid the banks altogether.

SCANDALS

It was not until the crash of 1987, and the later long recession, that the flood of money began to subside. The ebbing tide revealed the underlying dangers of the City like wreckage on the beach. Successive scandals showed up all the lack of regulation; how little the Bank of England was carrying out its duties behind that blank façade, and how inadequate was the law.

It was only because the crooked financier Ivan Boesky squealed in New

York that the British were alerted to the share-pushing of Ernest Saunders, the chairman of Guinness: and only the long-drawn-out trial revealed that the British legal system could not cope. When executives from County NatWest were charged with misusing funds, it took three years and nearly £40 million before the Appeal Court quashed the charges. And these trials were only the beginning. As the Guinness judge Sir Denis Henry put it:

> The power-driven, greed-fed, dishonest excesses of the 1980s have not proved to be the end of an unfortunate era but an introduction to worse since. We have to be able to deal with serious fraud: to deter it, to detect it, and to punish it.'[5]

In 1991 the Bank of England belatedly closed down BCCI, ruining thousands of mainly small, Asian depositors. A network of dishonest dealings in drugs, crime and corruption raised extreme doubts as to why BCCI was allowed to trade for so long. Sir Thomas Bingham, a High Court judge with a taste for investigation, began an exhaustive enquiry. He was hampered by the secrecy of the British banking laws which effectively concealed corruption and scared off some witnesses; but his findings were critical of the Bank of England, which had been told of BCCI's frauds by their auditors Price Waterhouse three months before they closed it down.

One dead man left behind a trail of disasters which revealed all the weakness of the regulators. In his lifetime Robert Maxwell was visibly a bruiser and megalomaniac who would stop at nothing; when I last met him he showed me round the huge office at the *Daily Mirror* which he had inherited as chairman from his predecessor Cecil King. I noted: 'more than ever a gorilla, with a bull neck: no sensitivity whatever.' 'To describe Bob Maxwell,' Lord Goodman advised me when I wrote my last *Anatomy*, 'you need someone from the meteorological office.' He was right: soon afterwards Hurricane Bob was hurtling through every citadel of power, knocking down their defences like cardboard boxes and exposing all their weaknesses to daylight. Bankers lent him hundreds of millions without serious security; directors approved fraudulent accounts; pension funds were wide open to plunder; and journalists could be paid to tell lies, or bullied by libel laws to suppress the truth.

Most seriously for the City, he revealed the shams behind much of the

---

[5] Child & Co. Lecture, June 17, 1992.

City's self-regulation. Maxwell had been described twenty years earlier by the Department of Trade as someone who could not be relied on 'to exercise proper stewardship of a publicly quoted company': yet there was no special watchfulness by official bodies who were supposed to safeguard the interests of shareholders or pensioners; including the Securities and Investment Board (SIB) and the Investment Management Regulatory Organisation (IMRO). And when thousands of ex-employees from Maxwell's paper the *Daily Mirror* were left without pensions worth £400 million they forced the embarrassing question: who was really responsible? The head of IMRO, George Nissen, whose father invented the wartime Nissen hut, honourably resigned, but the bankers lay low. The government lent the comical sum of £2.5 million and passed the buck to the City. The Bank of England came up with an emergency arbiter: Sir John Cuckney, a former MI5 man who had chaired the Royal Insurance company and the venture capital company 3i, who had his own leverage to persuade City companies to cough up. He warned that the City's reputation was at risk, and that government had its own sanctions: for it could exclude unco-operative banks from government projects and share-issues. 'How people react,' as Cuckney put it, 'is one of a number of factors which will be taken account of at future beauty parades.' In the end the government could not avoid the issue of morality.

The prime targets were the Big Four banks, who were hanging on to money which Maxwell had pledged against his loans: money which by any moral criteria was stolen property, which belonged to the pensioners. Only one bank, NatWest – significantly chaired by the non-banker Lord Alexander – offered cash, while the others kept quiet, ignominiously. For whatever their legal case, their moral position was untenable. And Maxwell was not just a freak in the system: he showed up all the irresponsibility, evasiveness and non-regulation which was undermining trust in the City.

10

Insurers

In June 1992 the weird structure of Lloyd's of London evoked a sense of dread, as the world's oldest insurance market prepared for its most critical annual meeting. The television cameras had rolled up to enjoy the unusual spectacle of paupers in pin-stripe: one obliged by repeatedly arriving on a penny-farthing with a notice: 'Impoverished name: give generously.' A sandwich-board man in straw hat patrolled outside the entrance with placards back and front: 'The End of the world is Nigh, but . . . best lunches at Beauchamps will be served all day.' I walked towards it without the usual reporter's relish of disasters; for I was also one of the 'Names' who had suddenly found their financial future at stake; and with 5,000 others I was trying to discover the extent of the damage.

Inside, the Names crowded into the building which now looked still more like a cathedral of money, with its concrete ribs soaring up to the high glass roof. In the centre of the nave, like an altar, was the canopy containing the old Lutine Bell – which has always been rung when a ship was sunk – as a reminder that this building is dedicated to risk. The see-through escalators perpetually rolled up and down, carrying the Names to the galleries round the nave, where they sat among the schoolboy desks and benches between the ledgers, copying machines and computer-screens.

It was a dramatic scene-change since I had first seen 'the Room' to be enrolled as a Name. Then the underwriters in their boxes round the galleries seemed to have the world's weather under control, as they allo-cated their risks with the visiting brokers, and talked nonchalantly about likely hurricanes, earthquakes or air-crashes in the 'catastrophe market'. Occasionally a visiting Name would look in on an underwriter to check on future profits. It was a club, run by professionals and trusted by outsiders.

Now the Names, the real bearers of the risk, had taken over the Room. Many of them had come from the country – farmers, widows, doctors, small businessmen. Many looked tense, haggard, sick. Yet in a macabre way the building had come to life: and it was revealing the true nature of the business on which it had been built: risk and catastrophe. It was as dramatic as the Merchant of Venice, with no end yet in sight: 'hath all his ventures failed, what not one hit . . . ?'

The Names exchanged notes anxiously about the dread numbers and names – Feltrim, Outhwaite, Gooda Walker – which had once seemed magical, and now send a chill. On one side of me a retired diplomat was hoping to recoup the heavy losses which wiped out his pension by writing a novel which would be called *Ruin*; on the other a widow, whose whole income had disappeared, explained that she had been working out her 'DFG' – distance from the gutter.

At 10.20 a.m. a magnificent flunkey rang the Lutine Bell twice to proclaim the annual meeting: but far more than a ship was sinking. The Council of Lloyd's trooped down the nave, followed by the chairman, David Coleridge, looking unlike the poet who was his ancestor: portly and smooth, but nervously fumbling with his papers.

At 10.30 a.m. the escalators stopped, the whole Room was silent, and the chairman began a long and anguished speech. His style was contrite. He announced losses of over £2 billion, an average of £60,000 per Name, but unevenly spread so that hundreds would be ruined. He talked about their 'despair, anger and bewilderment'. He admitted that Lloyd's had made some serious mistakes: they had expanded their capacity too fast in the eighties, and some underwriters had piled risk on risk. But they had learnt lessons bitterly. Now he was confident they could build a new future.

Then came the questions. Why did Mr Walker, when his agency Gooda Walker was collapsing, pay himself £300,000 for a year? Why should Names have to pay a levy after they've resigned? Why didn't agents realise how little income their Names had? Why must the chairman of Lloyd's always be an underwriter, with his own interests to protect, rather than an outside Name who represents the real risk? 'Some of us put all our trust in this institution,' said John Harris who was in several Gooda Walker syndicates: 'We feel totally betrayed.' The questions went on for five hours. The chairman went on sighing, looking still more penitent, and tried to offer some consolation: 'We do not force our members into bankruptcy.' But the rich Names who had built up large resources from past profits would not share the misery.

Some Names who had suffered seemed remarkably stoical. A few, particularly women, felt too anxious and fearful to intervene. Some like myself could derive comfort that others were much worse off. Few expected sympathy from outsiders. They had been warned about unlimited liability, with big risks but big rewards. They realised too late that they should not have trusted the professionals who told them so little. Yet as the fellow-sufferers exchanged disaster stories, amidst all their anger and hurt I noticed a certain pride in their moment of truth: that in a society which had become so impersonal and protected, they had been through their own hurricane, and were now prepared to take the consequences.

Lloyd's is an anachronism: an enclave of individuals in the midst of anonymous corporations as its assertive building implied. Ever since a group of ship-owners had begun exchanging risks in Lloyd's coffee-house in the seventeenth century, it had put its faith in mutual help between individuals who could trust each other. After the mid-nineteenth century, when other companies adopted limited liability, Lloyd's was unique; and it made the most of personal responsibility, by daring to insure every new risk from earthquakes to kidnap victims, and always paying up. It spread and reinsured the risks with skill and high profits, and after the Second World War Lloyd's profits with their tax-relief underpinned much of the life-style in British country-houses.

But the underwriters, brokers and agents were separated from the Names who took the biggest risks. The Lloyd's boys became a hereditary caste, a distinctive sub-tribe who could exchange favours, commissions and sometimes rackets – including discreet 'baby syndicates' which creamed off the best business – and some grew discreetly corrupt. They claimed to be self-regulating, like so many City institutions, but they were not. 'Their problem was that Labour never bothered to attack them,' their former chief executive Ian Hay Davison told me: 'because they thought it was only the rich stealing from the rich. So Lloyd's weren't under pressure to reform.'

By the late eighties they were facing tougher competition, particularly from America, and this made them accept more dangerous risks. And in 1987 a hurricane and an oil-rig disaster, together with past factory-pollution, produced unprecedented losses. As these cut a swathe through the country-houses, stricken Names were quick to blame the skulduggery of the insiders.

In its moment of truth, the original raw character of Lloyd's reemerged underneath the superstructure: it was still a group of individuals pledging their fortunes, with the same ultimate risks as the Merchant of Venice. In early centuries such risks were not confined to insurance: they had ruined thousands of investors (including my great-grandfather) in banks and other businesses before joint stock companies had established limited liability. But only Lloyd's had survived. Its old motto, Fidentia, now rang hollow, adapted to 'Fiddle-entia'. But in that loss of trust it was not alone. The motto of the Stock Exchange – My Word is My Bond – rang almost as hollow. In ten years the old assumptions of the gentlemanly clubs, the unwritten rules and friendships which ruled the City, had been swept away. Laws and lawyers had moved in.

The issue of personal responsibility would not go away. It was the ability of individuals to pass the buck which lay behind all the City scandals, whether in the banks, the boardrooms or the Bank of England. The insurance business was based on the principle of sharing responsibility, but the buck still had to stop somewhere.

INSURANCE COMPANIES

Lloyd's made up only a small proportion of Britain's total insurance, most of which was handled by giant companies. These were the ten biggest 'Non-Life' companies (excluding Life Assurance), graded by their premium income in 1992, with the previous year's losses. Their chairmen, mostly City figures from outside the insurance bureaucracy, were supposed to bring a wider perspective, but it remained a self-contained world.

Company	Chairman	Premium income	Previous year's losses
Royal	Sir John Cuckney	3.6 bn	−726 m
General Accident	Earl of Airlie	3.0 bn	−461 m
Sun Alliance	Henry Lambert	2.5 bn	−550 m
Commercial Union	Nicholas Baring	2.4 bn	−344 m
Guardian Royal Exchange	C. E. A. Hambro	2.0 bn	−460 m
Eagle Star Holdings	Michael Butt	1.6 bn	−475 m
Norwich Union	Michael Falcon	1.1 bn	−292 m
Prudential Corp	Sir Brian Corby	1.0 bn	−317 m
Municipal Mutual	Maurice Stonefrost	572 m	−173 m
Cornhill Insurance	C. G. Burrows	504 m	−39 m

Many of them had suffered proportionately greater losses than Lloyd's and been at least as rash. The Prudential – whose vast Life business makes it far the biggest overall – made an absurd blunder in the early eighties when they bought up chains of estate agents, about which they knew little. By 1991, as property slumped, they had to sell them off at a loss of £300 million. Just at that time the Pru's chief executive, Mick Newmarch, the great bear of insurance, had his salary increased by 43 per cent to £544,000 a year. There was an outcry from shareholders who thought that the boss should share some of the pain; but the board was immune. While Lloyd's Names were being ruined, corporate managers were much more protected for their mistakes.

It is the Life companies which have become the real centre of the argument about financial responsibility. These businesses hold far the biggest funds for investment. The working men's clubs which had grown up in the nineteenth century, collecting weekly savings to provide pensions, had gradually accumulated and invested such vast sums from their millions of policy-holders that they became the biggest shareholders in industry. These were the biggest Life companies in 1991 (half of them are also among the biggest Non-Life companies), with their chairmen, life funds and premium income. Between them they are responsible for £130 billion.

Company	Chairman	Life fund	Premium income
Prudential	Sir Brian Corby	32.5 bn	5.0 bn
Standard Life	N. Lessels	18.4 bn	3.0 bn
Norwich Union	M. G. Falcon	17.4 bn	2.4 bn
Legal & General	Sir James Ball	14.8 bn	2.6 bn
Commercial Union	Nicholas Baring	9.7 bn	1.1 bn
Scottish Widows'	C. H. Black	9.4 bn	1.2 bn
Sun Alliance	Henry Lambert	7.4 bn	861 m
Friends' Provident	Lord Jenkin of Roding	7.3 bn	1.0 bn
Sun Life	P. J. Grant	7.2 bn	999 m
Eagle Star	Michael Butt	6.8 bn	950 m

The Pru, with almost twice the annual income to invest as the next, is still run from its Victorian red-brick cathedral in Holborn – on the edge of the square mile of the City from which it remains deliberately aloof. Over three decades its chief executives have gradually faced up to their role as key actors in the control of industry: they have begun to intervene in extreme crises when companies were visibly mismanaged, or when warring directors ask investors to take sides, and have become far more closely involved in investigating companies and their managers. Today many chairmen and directors see the Pru's chief executive Mick Newmarch as the most powerful single figure in industry.

The fund managers of the Life companies and pension funds – cryptically called 'the Institutions' – have emerged as the ultimate wielders of financial power and controllers of industry. In the late seventies the Labour government appointed the ex-prime minister Harold Wilson to chair a Commission on the City which gave special attention to the power of pension funds. 'They could be more powerful than the cabinet, and they leak a lot less,' Wilson told me; and in his memoirs he stressed their dramatic emergence:

> The growth of pension funds during and since the middle 1970s has created the biggest revolution in the financial scene in this century. Surprisingly it was almost totally unperceived by political and even financial commentators until very recently.[1]

Wilson was struck by the unaccountability of the young fund managers, the 'beardless boys' as he called them; but he saw that they were in a dilemma: 'if they interfere in industry they're exerting a power which was given to them for quite other reasons; and if they don't interfere they're accused of having power without responsibility. They can't win.'

The concentrated power of the big fund managers offended the Conservative philosophy of the eighties which was dedicated to individual choice. For most of the millions of policy-holders and future pensioners had no choice about how their savings should be invested: while the tax laws virtually obliged the self-employed to put their savings into funds rather than choose their own investments.

In spite of this managerial responsibility and experience, pensions were not necessarily invested for the benefit of the pensioners. Unscrupulous entrepreneurs could invest their employees' pension funds for their own advantage; and a raider who bid for a company often saw access to the fund as a critical asset. There had been plenty of abuses of this pension-power in the past; but it was not until Robert Maxwell succeeded in plundering £400 million from the *Daily Mirror* fund and leaving the

---

[1] Harold Wilson: *The Final Term*, Weidenfeld & Nicholson, London, 1979, p. 146.

pensioners ruined that the criminal irresponsibility of the system was laid bare.

The same irresponsibility was reflected in the dreary buildings which pensions indirectly financed and which dominate the city centres. Victorian investors filled London with landmarks, from Tower Bridge to St Pancras Station to the Pru itself, which can still amaze tourists and sell postcards: but few new monuments have attracted visitors over recent decades, least of all during the boom years of the eighties. London has only a few business palaces, like the Shell Centre, which were commissioned by the company which inhabits them: most of the shapeless blocks have been speculations by developers using capital from pension funds, which are then rented to big companies. The government likewise commissions very few buildings, like the British Library, and normally rents space in inappropriate developers' towers, like the deathly Marsham Street offices of the Board of Trade which overhang Westminster. Those bleak rectangles round St Paul's are reminders of the anonymous processes which brought them into being. The more daring new apparitions, like Canary Wharf or Lloyd's, tend to become associated with disaster.

The most serious charge against fund managers is their lack of interest in the long-term prospects of companies. While they represent the interests of employees who may have twenty or thirty years to wait for their pensions, they are constantly competing with each other from day to day, anxiously watching the quarterly earnings of corporations, and looking for quick gains. The Germans and Japanese are more effectively insulated: with the help of their banks, and cross-holdings of shares, they are prepared to plan twenty or thirty years ahead; as the Japanese banks showed in financing the Channel Tunnel. But the British insurance companies, behind their images of rock-like permanence, have set the pace for short-term profit-making which characterises financial management today.

The short horizons of fund managers inevitably affect the horizons of industrialists, though many deny it: they encourage take-overs and discourage long-term research and projects which take a long time to yield results. And the hectic dealing of the fund managers has joined the faster pace in both Britain and America, where competing investments and interest-rates in the global market place have sent ever-larger sums chasing short-term gains. This has prevented bankers and investors from addressing critical long-term problems, including resolving the debt crisis and safeguarding the environment. 'We define out of existence certain types of problems that have a longer time-cycle...' John Read, the chairman of Citibank, told me: 'There are lots of problems that you can't get done in ten years, but which you could very well address in twenty-five.'

In the last few years the end of the long booms on stock-markets has forced investors to take a longer view, through pessimism about the short-term. Sir Alastair Morton of Eurotunnel ascribes part of his company's success in raising funds to the timing of the share-issue just after the Crash of 1987: as he explained, 'all investments are long term after the market collapses.'[2] The long recession has encouraged pension fund managers to move out of industrial shares and into bonds and government stocks which provide a safer return. At the same time new laws have enabled individuals to opt out of corporate pension schemes, to make their own choice. And a new generation of fund managers has begun to provide a wider choice of personal investment, including Green funds and ethical funds which keep out of tobacco, arms companies or polluters.

But there remains a clear contradiction between the calculations of money managers and the long-term needs of industry. And while the British are very successful devising and selling funds, pensions, insurance policies or shares, they are even less interested in Britain's industrial base.

[2] Speech to Birmingham Polytechnic, June 9, 1992.

I I

Industrialists

Through the eighties the motorways gave spectacular glimpses of new prosperity, as business palaces, parks and campuses rose up like fantasy universities: high roofs with wide eaves, gabled towers, triangular windows, gaunt glass rectangles or shiny towers which could have all come from the same giant's toyshop. They look triumphant compared to the crumbling old manufacturing sheds in the towns.

I had often wondered what went on behind these romantic façades, and eventually I had a chance to see inside this brave new world, as a judge of architectural prizes for new buildings. The first building was a chaste, pale-grey tower near Swindon railway station, part of a 'dedicated complex' which might have been dropped down from Scandinavia. Swindon once built locomotives for the Great Western Railway but now the old workshops alongside the main line are empty and decaying. The local council was determined to attract new industry and become the 'fastest growing city in Europe'. Inside the complex, 2,300 people, mostly women, were filing, phoning and tapping into computers in long white modular rooms. They were handling pensions, insurance policies and financial transactions, as expertly as their grandfathers would have handled boilers or pistons. They seemed under a trance in this rarefied workshop with its air-conditioned hum, with only 'beverage points' and a garish notice-board to break the white spell.

The second building was a dark mirror-glass slab in a business park near Bristol. From the outside it betrayed nothing except elaborate security, like an avant-garde jail. Inside were seventy-five people, all dedicated to looking after banks of computers cosseted at precisely the right temperature, with their own generators to ensure a steady current. The rows of white and blue boxes kept blinking day and night endlessly transmitting and receiving millions of messages from America and Europe, doing the work of thousands of clerks. They turned out to be controlled, not by the staff in the building, but from the headquarters of a global insurance company 140 miles away.

The third was a low Japanese-looking building, in the middle of the Wiltshire countryside, black-and-white like an overgrown chalet, surrounded by parkland but air-conditioned and sealed to keep out any breeze. Inside was an ultra-modern training centre teaching young self-employed how to sell insurance and pensions. The building generated drama and commitment, with theatrical lighting, lecture rooms with glass walls for monitoring, banks of computer screens, telephones, microphones. There were small cinemas for programmed lectures with automatic blinds to cut out the daylight; and bedrooms as functional as sleeping-cars. The whole place buzzed with the language of high-pressure salesmanship; with role-playing, training modes, body language, total quality management and up-front commitment – commitment above all to the 'product'.

The products are not solid objects to touch and see. They are all digits: sums of money representing insurance policies and pensions, profits and commissions. For these new palaces all enshrine the booming industry of financial services which has transformed southern England. It is the triumph of a new age-group which intimidates elders. 'This is something we leave to a younger generation,' said the chairman of an insurance company to me with a wry smile. It is a remarkable new industrial revolution which has risen from the ruins of manufacture. But it raises questions. Are these products genuinely productive, creating wealth or just shuffling it around? Can Britain export them to buy manufactured products in return? And does this activity – highly centralised, programmed, mass-produced – represent a liberation of the individual, or a new servitude?

City people and ministers insist that financial services are just as productive as manufacture. But many industrialists know that the British have lost interest in real production. 'What will the service industries be servicing,' asked Lord Weinstock, giving evidence to the House of Lords Select Committee on Overseas Trade in 1985, 'when there is no hardware, where no wealth is actually being produced? We will be servicing presumably the production of wealth by others.' 'I am bearish about the future for industrial manufacturing in the UK,' Sir John Harvey-Jones, the usually bullish chairman of ICI, told the same committee. With his long hair, loud ties and giggles, Harvey-Jones became the maverick champion of British industry in the eighties and later a television folk-hero as 'troubleshooter'. But he remained exasperated by the British prejudice against industry.

Behind much of the apathy towards industry lies the simple question of money. As the City offered both more prestige and higher salaries, the manufacturing managers fell further behind. At the beginning of the decade they faced a harsh world of recession, high interest-rates and government neglect. Companies took pride in becoming 'leaner and fitter', but some became as lean as skeletons before they disappeared altogether. Corporate chairmen rapidly changed their self-image: in the seventies they boasted how many people they employed; now it was how many they had fired. To describe a businessman as ruthless used to be libellous: now it was high praise. As the surviving companies came out of the recession of the early eighties they became much more profitable, with higher productivity; but usually because of fewer workers, rather than more production; total industrial output hardly increased. By the end of the eighties they were back in the doldrums, facing a still worse recession and much stiffer competition from abroad.

PRIVATEERS AND BARONS

Manufacture was in decline, but the private sector was boosted by a gigantic change of ownership, from successive denationalisations. Remarkably, this new 'popular capitalism' happened largely by accident, and had no part in Mrs Thatcher's first manifesto. Sir Martin Jacomb (then at Kleinwort's) who was charged with selling off British Telecom, found that he could not raise enough funds from international investors, so appealed to the public through an unprecedented advertising campaign to people who had never owned shares. To the surprise and delight of the government, it was a spectacular success.

So began the privatising revolution. Between 1979 and 1988 public sector employees fell from 9 per cent to 5 per cent of the workforce – which did more to weaken the militant unions than government policy. More importantly it enriched the Treasury without raising taxes. With the sale of council houses and other local assets, the sell-off constituted the biggest change of ownership (says the historian Keith Middlemass) since the dissolution of the monasteries or the plunder of Royalist estates after the Civil War.[1]

---

[1] Middlemass, *op. cit.*, p. 363.

THE TOP 25 BRITISH COMPANIES

Company	Chairman or chief executive	Background	Turnover (1990–1) £,000
1 Royal Dutch/Shell	Sir Peter Holmes	Cambridge; Company	59,416,000
2 British Petroleum	David Simon	Cambridge; MBA	41,711,000
3 Unilever	Michael Perry	Oxford; Marketing	22,258,000
4 BAT Industries	Sir Patrick Sheehy	Company	15,027,000
5 British Telecom*	Ian Vallance	Oxford; Company	13,154,000
6 ICI	Sir Denys Henderson	Lawyer	12,906,000
7 British Aerospace*	John Cahill	ex-BTR	10,540,000
8 British Gas*	Robert Evans	Engineer	9,491,000
9 Grand Metropolitan	Sir Allen Sheppard	Company	9,394,000
10 Sumitomo UK	Iwao Nishiumi	(in Japan)	8,265,000
11 Sainsbury	David Sainsbury	Family	7,813,000
12 Hanson	Lord Hanson	Family	7,153,000
13 BTR	Sir Owen Green	Accountant	6,742,000
14 Ford	Ian McAllister	Company	6,732,000
15 Tesco	Sir Ian MacLaurin	Company	6,346,000
16 Marks & Spencer	Richard Greenbury	Company	5,744,800
17 Esso UK	Sir Archibald Forster	Engineer	5,401,000
18 General Electric	Lord Weinstock	Statistician	5,252,800
19 Allied Lyons	Michael Jackaman	Cambridge; Company	5,113,000
20 British Steel*	Sir Robert Scholey	Engineer	5,113,000
21 P & O	Lord Sterling	Stockbroker	5,036,000
22 Marubeni UK	Hideo Tanaka	(in Japan)	4,994,158
23 British Airways*	Lord King		4,838,000
24 SmithKline Beecham	Henry Wendt	Company	4,764,000
25 Argyll	Alistair Grant	Cambridge; Company	4,757,500

* = ex-nationalised.

It also created new barons. The newly-privatised chairmen, led by Sir Ian MacGregor of British Steel and the Coal Board and Lord King of British Airways, became the heroes of capitalism, moving from one board-room to another. They were responsible for giant companies which are among the biggest in the country (see above). But they also raised problems in their relationships with their new shareholders, to whom they were unwilling to be accountable – particularly over the question of their salaries. The democracy of shareholders was looking as ineffective as the democracy of voters.

Many of the privatised chairmen relished a buccaneering style which became part of the mythology of the eighties. Mrs Thatcher enjoyed promoting adventurous businessmen rather as Queen Elizabeth I promoted Sir Francis Drake; and they made the most of her favouritism, impressing underlings by implying a private line to the top. Some have survived into the nineties: the new chief executive of British Airports Authority in 1991, Sir John Egan, the former head of Jaguar Cars, is an abrasive entrepreneur who swiftly replanned the projected new Terminal 5 at Heathrow, with more shops and fewer seats.

Mrs Thatcher's departure upset her barons: after her fall Lord Sterling entertained her in New York in August 1991, on board his new P & O cruise liner the *Regal Princess*, with tributes from Henry Kissinger and Ronald Reagan on videotape; but the Americans now admire her more than the British, and business bluster looks less effective in Major's Britain. In 1991 Lord King was outraged because British Airways' rival Virgin Atlantic, run by Richard Branson, had been awarded precious new air routes; and he tactlessly announced that he was stopping British Airways' annual donation of £40,000 to the Conservative Party. He was so easily slapped down by the Minister of Transport Malcolm Rifkind that his glory evaporated: his private line had gone dead. Now he has been succeeded by his chief executive Colin Marshall, a notably modest and self-effacing master-manager: and it is Branson who is now flying the skull and cross-bones, suing British Airways for defamation while he calls for more air routes.

The privateers were naturally impatient of regulation. They were profit-seekers who used formidable lobbying or bullying power to get their own way. But private monopolies were obviously open to exploitation (which was why Imperial Airways, the forerunner of British Airways, had originally been nationalised in 1939). Their profits depended on how much they charged to the consumer; while the water boards, the last and most controversial asset to be privatised, owned precious waterfronts which developers could exploit at great cost to the environment.

But the government in their eagerness to privatise had given surprisingly little thought to how to regulate these key industries: regulation was a dirty word in the right-wing vocabulary and many economists including *The Economist* expected it to fade away as competition developed. The government set up new bodies to supervise state monopolies, led by Oftel and Ofgas to oversee telecommunications and gas; but their powers were not properly defined so they depended heavily on the personality of their directors. Sir James McKinnon of Ofgas, a combative accountant, was a consumers' champion who enjoyed creative tension, and he showed his mettle when he forced Robert Evans of British Gas to reduce his charges in 1992. But there was more scepticism about Oftel, first under Sir Bryan Carsberg, a professor of accounting, then under his deputy Bill Wigglesworth. For British Telecom is spectacularly profitable, largely because of high rates for phone calls, particularly international calls which are maintained by a cartel; they have both less regulation and less competition than the Japanese privatised telephone system NTT. The chairman of British Telecom, Ian Vallance, will naturally fight to defend the profits. But he is at odds both with consumers who resent the high charges, and shareholders who resent the high salaries.

The more privatisers were glorified, the more the remaining public industries were demoralised. The most visible decay has been in transport. In the eighties the French and Germans had been discovering the benefits of high-speed trains which could link city centres without the disruptions of airports and traffic-jams; and they developed a new infrastructure (a French word) across the continent. But the British Conservatives were exasperated by British Rail, and Mrs Thatcher refused to travel by train: she saw the car as the champion of free choice against the nationalised trains, and her government poured money into motorways to satisfy the car-and-truck lobby, the British Road Federation. They wanted to privatise the whole railway system but couldn't work out how, so the board of British Rail remained scapegoats without the funds to redeem themselves. In 1990 a new chairman from Shell, Sir Bob Reid, a combative and highly-paid Scot, arrived full of steam. But politically he was shunted into a siding; and even after John Major succeeded Thatcher the government still favoured roads against rail: in 1991 they allocated £2 billion to widen the London orbital road, the M25, but nothing more to the railways or Underground network which could relieve the congestion. By 1989 the roads were taking 83 per cent of Britain's freight, at fearful cost to the environment: in the ten years to 1989 pollution from road transport went up from 884 million tonnes to 1,298 million tonnes of nitrogen oxides.

The London Underground has become still more demoralised: once the envy of the world, it has become a national disgrace, notorious for fires, squalor, lack of trains and violence. The new chairman in 1989, Wilfrid Newton, appeared hopeful: originally from Johannesburg, he had been chairman of the Hong Kong Mass Transit Railway, one of the most efficient in the world; but in London he was soon bogged down by antiquated trains, and shortage of funds. A serious lack of management and accountability led to buying expensive new lifts and escalators which did not work and showing a general contempt for the passenger. In contrast with the business palaces aboveground these underground slums became more like a Third World city; and Docklands provided a caricature of the imbalance between private and public investment, with the empty skyscraper of Canary Wharf still waiting for an Underground rail route to reach it.

A NEW CLASS?

Meanwhile the privatised chairmen were setting the pace for record salaries, while warning their workers against inflationary wage-claims. Ian Vallance of British Telecom received a rise of £50,000 a year in 1991, stimulating other chairmen to join the race even when their profits were falling in the recession. The companies explained that the salaries were fixed by the remuneration committee of non-executive directors, and that chairmen had to be highly-paid to compete in a global market place. But exorbitant American salaries were already provoking a political outcry and action by the SEC in Washington, and British chairmen offered no evidence of being wooed by Americans.

By 1992 the greed of British directors had led to a confrontation with the managers. 'If they continue to reward themselves far more than their employees they'll have to answer for it,' warned Roger Young, the new director of the British Institute of Management. But they did not answer for it and the director of the Institute of Directors, Peter Morgan, counter-blasted at his annual rally: 'to assume that directors' earnings should go up in good times and down in bad times is about as useful as paying the weather man depending on the weather.' The Archbishop of Canterbury, George Carey, hurled a thunderbolt: he warned a congregation of businessmen in Derby that God could curse the rich who did not feed the poor, and explained that the purpose of industry was not to 'make profits for shareholders, nor to create salaries and wages for the industrial community,' but 'to serve people by creating things of use and value to them.' But the Archbishop was naive about money and Peter Morgan was unrepentant: 'I prefer Adam Smith to the Archbishop on the question of understanding the purpose of business.' And the Bishop of Oxford, Richard Harries, weighed in to explain that 'Christ is Lord of the markets and exchanges of the world as much as of its monasteries and churches.'

Directors' salaries were bringing to a head the whole question of accountability to shareholders or employees. The non-executive directors who approve the salaries are supposed to represent wider interests, but they often turn out to be friends of the chairman, whom they have no wish to offend: they are paid an average of £15,000 a year. In 1992 Sir Adrian Cadbury, the former chocolate chairman, produced a report on 'corporate governance' which found that 'up to 80 per cent of the appointments to the boards of large British companies are still made on the old boy network'. Some of the boards have *very* old boys, well into their seventies, who are glad to have a job. Cadbury insisted that shareholders should have much more information about their directors' pay; but not that they should vote over it: and he proposed a voluntary code, a form of self-regulation which the tougher boards could ignore without much trouble.

The high-handedness of British boards goes far back into their history, and they have always tended to see managers as an inferior species. As Ronald Grierson (a director of GEC) described it: 'In the US and on the European continent management is top-dog for both policy and implementation – and enjoys the accompanying prestige – while boards, though possessing the ultimate deterrent, confine themselves in practice to ensuring that management does not run amok.'[2] On the continent boards are also more likely to see themselves responsible not just to their shareholders but to their employees and consumers. And the most recent management experts, including the British guru Professor Charles Handy, have suggested that a company's long-term success depends on a healthy 'corporate culture' which takes full note of customers and employees as well as shareholders.

But salaries of many directors and chairmen have been pushed up to record levels, which suggests serious class warfare. There have always been feudal tendencies within British industry: in the thirties Lord McGowan treated ICI as his fiefdom (even while he bankrupted himself with wild speculation); and in the sixties Lord Chandos regarded

---

[2] Letter to *Financial Times*, June 10, 1992.

Associated Electrical Industries as his private estate while its profits declined. The new chairmen are much more professional and meritocratic, but they still see themselves as establishing a new aristocracy. The hierarchies and rituals of British office-life still show some resemblances to Victorian country-houses, with private lifts in place of grand staircases, chauffeurs instead of coachmen, secretaries instead of nannies or maids, and butlers to open dining-room doors. In the high-tax years of the sixties and seventies the luxurious company perks including golf courses, yachts and country-clubs were explained as compensation for high taxes. But though taxes went down in the eighties directors still wanted more money and more perks, separating themselves still further from their workers and often their managers. They have set themselves up as a class apart from normal society, competing with each other in their own league table, defying the democracy of the shareholders. As civil servants, judges and ministers find their salaries constrained in the battle against inflation the chairmen and directors are still more exposed, outside any society but their own.

It is a long way from the managerial revolution which was the wisdom of the sixties. American theories about scientific management and rational models still prevailed in Britain through the seventies. 'It was a world in which people were seen as machines; leadership was something best left to the generally discredited military,' wrote John Banham, director of the CBI in 1992: 'it was the era of the model builder, the optimizer.'[3] But the early eighties showed a shift from this 'tyranny of reason' summed up by the American book *In Search of Excellence*, by Peters and Waterman, in 1982. After inspecting successful companies the authors decided that the assumptions of scientific management, including the importance of size, total control and analysis, were no longer useful disciplines, and that effective managers were as much concerned with the aesthetic and intuitive process of pathfinding as with decision making. They concluded that 'we have to stop overdoing things on the rational side'.

By the nineties British managers as well as American were giving more emphasis to leadership than reason. 'Perhaps management is not a science after all,' wrote Henry Strage, a veteran of McKinsey's in London: 'though some of us in the 1950s and later tried to persuade ourselves that it was.'[4]

---

[3] *Milestones in Management*, edited by Henry M. Strage, Blackwell, London, 1992, p. 368.
[4] Strage, *ibid.*, p. ix.

The cult of leadership, which had been suspect since Hitler, was now coming back into fashion. It was true that inspiration and flair had been too long neglected, and that business like politics needed some charisma at the top. But the earlier business autocrats like Deterding of Shell, who supported Hitler in the thirties, could easily develop into megalomaniacs without effective restraints – which many British boards still have not achieved.

And macho leadership is less appealing to many employees further down, particularly to women managers striving to gain recognition in a male atmosphere. When in March 1992 the Institute of Directors polled its women directors (who make up 8 per cent of their members), a third claimed direct experience of sex discrimination, and three-quarters believed women were discriminated against in the work-place. Another study showed that the make-up of boards had been little changed by the supposed social upheavals: the typical director was a fifty-two-year-old chartered accountant, probably a golfer from a grammar school: his most likely club was the RAC or the MCC. Out of 20,000 directors and senior executives, only 426 were women.[5] The most striking gains for women in business have been as chief executives' secretaries, whose average pay in central London has gone up from £11,200 to £18,600 in the five years to 1992.[6] They are now way ahead of teachers and civil engineers, but they contribute to the new emphasis on leadership.

The problems of containing leadership were dramatically played out in June 1992 in the boardroom of BP, the British oil company with a history of autocratic bosses, including the Scots tyrant Lord Strathalmond whose arrogance helped to lose them Iran in 1951. In 1990 the board rashly chose a new chairman and chief executive, Robert Horton, who had already developed a domineering style in America where he swung an axe through the staff of BP's subsidiary Sohio. Back in London Horton faced daunting problems: a heavy debt burden, an oil-price too low to pay for the huge commitments, and the legendary BP bureaucracy which preferred to have three people doing one job. He soon swung his axe again, moved the headquarters back into its earlier Edwardian building, and instituted a bold 'Project 1990' which pressed managers to simplify and take more responsibility. But at the same time he cultivated his own power, demoralising his colleagues; and while BP's profits were collapsing in the recession,

[5] Arthur Andersen Corporate Register, *Financial Times*, April 7, 1992.
[6] Reward Group report, August 13, 1992.

he insisted on still paying out dividends which cut into the reserves.

Luckily BP, with its memories of tyrants, has unusually strong outside directors, including foreign industrialists and the former head of Barings, Lord Ashburton (formerly Sir John Baring), a tall hereditary banker who commands authority in the City. He soon took against Horton's autocracy, and was joined by the other directors. Only two years after appointing Horton, they fired him, replacing him as chief executive with his more discreet rival David Simon, and as chairman with Ashburton, whose moment had now come: a banker had once again outfoxed an engineer. The share price promptly fell by 14 per cent, and six weeks later the dividend was cut. The coup at BP was rightly hailed as a triumph of corporate democracy, but it was a victory for far-sighted directors rather than short-term shareholders: and it had depended on having enough members of the board who were not afraid of the boss.

RAIDERS V. CORPOCRATS

The greatest challenge to the managerial revolution came from the incursions of a small band of raiders, who claimed to be liberating the shareholders from the stultifying rule of the managers or 'corpocrats', and threatened to turn the biggest companies inside out. The epic battles led by mythological figures like Lord Hanson and Sir James Goldsmith made marvellous stories, and they lit up the problems of the control of industry, at the heart of the financial anatomy. But their achievements were never as glorious as they looked.

Goldsmith was their prophet, a glamorous billionaire, a friend of Thatcher, who seemed to have walked out of a nineteenth-century novel. He depicted himself as a restless spirit whose destiny was to upset the peace of the world. 'Dynamism is usually the result of disequilibrium,' he told me: 'My disequilibrium comes from the very simple reason that I'm a foreigner over here. I'm a Jew to Catholics, a Catholic to Jews, an Englishman to the French and a Frenchman to the English.' He relished the role of predator in the jungle of business, and promised shareholders to restore the 'life-giving link between ownership and management'.[7]

Corporate directors and managers found it hard to compete with such exciting appeals to their shareholders, whom they had preferred to forget;

[7] Hearings on Monopolies: House of Representatives, Washington, November 18, 1986.

and they fought back uneasily. The two sides confronted each other at an extraordinary debate inside the Bank of England in 1989, on the motion that 'contested bids tend to be bad for industry', with an audience of a hundred financiers and industrialists which I managed to infiltrate: for me it was a moment of truth. Goldsmith, in fighting form, insisted that raiders in the past could have saved many dying British industries by cutting back surplus fat: 'the owner wants value: the manager wants size.' Captains of industry led by Sir John Harvey-Jones explained the need for continuity, but conceded that the threat of raiders helped to shake up companies. The industrialists expectantly waited to hear Mick Newmarch of the Prudential, the biggest single investor in industry: he explained how he wished there were less drastic correctives to bad management, but reluctantly saw no alternative to raiders. He came to his final point: but there was a terrible silence. The debate in the end proved a pushover: the raiders won their case with a show of hands giving four to one against the motion. Goldsmith told me he had expected to lose. It was an alarming insight into the weakness of Britain's industrialists.

A few months later Goldsmith himself went back into the fray, mounting a raid which promised to 'unbundle' British American Tobacco – which failed, but shook up its victim. And soon afterwards Lord Hanson prepared for a bid for ICI, which provided an epic challenge – the biggest British raider stalking the biggest manufacturing company with a proud history of research. The current chairman of ICI Sir Denys Henderson, a Scots lawyer and salesman, swiftly reorganised his company, pruning its research, which he said he would have done anyway, and commissioning a public relations campaign to promote ICI: he had his own doubts about the future of very large companies, and thought that conglomerates like Hanson would turn into dinosaurs. Hanson eventually gave up his bid with some loss of face, but with a profit of £40 million on his ICI shares. ICI soon afterwards did what Hanson would have done: split the company into two.

Both these big raids suggested that managers try harder with a wolf at the door. But the casualties include long-term development. The raiders insisted that their bids only cut out wastage, and that the valuable research is reflected in the market-price; but the value of long, patient research is very hard to assess and very expensive to fund. And the raids revealed all the underlying conflict between the short-term priorities of the City and the long-term needs of industry – needs which Japanese competitors could pursue for twenty years ahead, with no risks of disruption from share-holders or raiders. The raiders left big companies unsure of their identities, both in Britain and America. For if they must provide quick profits for shareholders, to fend off raiders, how can they present themselves as the guardians of broader interests, whether as planners for the future, patrons of communities, or sponsors of the arts? They also encouraged a war-like atmosphere in the boardrooms. The teams of lawyers, bankers and consult-ants on each side loved to talk about war chests, dawn raids, salvos and counter-salvos; to hold midnight meetings in war rooms with the camaraderie and smell of battle. They were in no mood to open up to other groups, let alone the other gender.

The raiders came from a much more international context than most companies they raided: they could reach across the globe, armed with their bank loans and financial wizardry, to bid for settled companies which had grown up in their community. The end product of the process of raiding and merging is the multinational corporation which overlaps national borders, run by a new species of businessman, multinational man, which I have written about in other books.[8] He has extraordinary migratory habits, carrying his office in his briefcase, his suit over his shoulder, his car-keys in his belt, migrating in jumbos between almost identical L-shaped rooms in computerised hotels, with no fixed abode. When a banker was asked: 'What is your address?' he replied, 'Just 747.' Measured by mileage and passport-stamps he is more cosmopolitan than the earlier business traveller on trains and steamships; but he has far less contact with other walks of life. He can spend two days in a windowless basement in the convention hotel near the airport, with no time to escape to the real city, before flying straight back to his base. And the recession made companies question the need for these expensive journeys when videos, conference calls and faxes could carry facts and figures instantly round the world.

Global man is not really very global: the further and faster he travels, the more his life is circumscribed and conditioned by his corporate col-leagues. In the sixties many economists and even chairmen talked about companies without frontiers: mergers across borders like that between British Dunlop and Italian Pirelli were seen as part of a new era of com-

---

[8] *The Sovereign State of ITT*: Hodder & Stoughton, London, 1973; *The Seven Sisters*: Hodder & Stoughton, London, 1975; *The Arms Bazaar*: Hodder & Stoughton, 1977.

panies without nationalities. But the rubber-merger soon came unstuck and most multinationals remain firmly based in one nation. ICI has become much less Imperial, more European; but its board remains emphatically British, and its rivalry with the German chemical giants is an extension of old national rivalries. And in their global clashes all the multinationals look to their own governments for privileges and protection.

SMALL BUSINESS

The smallest businesses run by individuals remain the essential basis of every country's commercial energy and creativity; and they can have no doubt about their responsibility to either shareholders or customers. Small businessmen have been traditionally neglected and under-represented in British politics, and they looked with new hopes to Mrs Thatcher – the first post-war prime minister to champion the shopkeeping class from which she came. New shops, services or restaurants were the outward signs of how much past enterprise had been suppressed, and brought a new choice and variety to the richer cities. The numbers of self-employed people in Britain went up by 57 per cent in the decade to 1990, to nearly 3.25 million. In the seventies Britain had many fewer self-employed than the European average; by the end of the eighties the gap had almost closed: 12 per cent compared to 13 per cent in the EC.[9]

But their success was fragile, and after 1989 they were caught in a trap. Interest-rates shot up, creditors delayed payments and banks foreclosed. In 1990 29,000 companies went bankrupt, in 1991 48,000. Small companies lacked lobbying power against their big rivals or customers. Banks which had lent hundreds of millions to Robert Maxwell closed down small businesses that owed a few thousand. Big customers withheld payment for months, accumulating the interest while bankrupting their victims – and the government offered no redress. It showed the true ruthlessness of the brute power of big business against small. In the four years to 1990 the debts owed to privately-owned business in England and Wales doubled in value (allowing for inflation), and the delays in payment were far longer than on the continent: the average debt took fifty-one days after the

[9] *Social Trends*, 1992, p. 75; Department of Employment: *Small Firms in Britain*, 1992.

normal thirty-day terms, compared to thirty-four days in Italy, twenty-eight in France and eighteen in Sweden. By 1990 nearly one-in-five privately-owned firms were under threat because of late payment, according to a CBI survey. When Michael Mates introduced a private member's bill in February 1990 to enforce payment of interest on debts it was supported by 230 MPs but not by the government.[10]

The most obvious victim has been the best loved British social institution: the village pub, which was still more damaged by muddled government policies meant to protect it. The Monopolies Commission reported on the excessive power of the big brewers and the Department of Trade decided that they could not own more than 2,000 'tied houses'; but the brewers saw that as a chance to rationalise their business, replacing long-serving tenants with their own managers, and selling off their least profitable pubs – often much-loved country inns – while offering them loans if they undertook to sell only their beer. When the recession and breathalysers deterred drinkers, the small pub-owners lost money and loans were withdrawn. By May 1992 the pub-owners' body, the National Licensed Victuallers Association, had lost nearly half its 15,000 members in two years, and was dissolved. They were, said their President, Roy Peddie, 'quite simply a victim of the ravage and rape of our industry which we have witnessed over the last year.' 'An essential part of British life is becoming a rat race,' said their chief executive, John Overton. 'It is good old-style landlords and traditional hostelries that are suffering.'[11] The evidence can be seen all through the British countryside.

Recession inevitably weakened the individual businesses including pubs, shops or restaurants while some big chains like Sainsbury or Marks and Spencer increased their profits. The pressure to conform grew. The motorways were dominated by the filling-stations and shops of the giant oil companies and the endless chain of eateries and hotels controlled by Lord Forte, including Travelodge, the Little Chef and the Happy Eater – a uniformity more extreme than the American mass-culture which the British had so long mocked.

[10] Forum of Private Business, Knutsford, Cheshire, 1992.
[11] *The Times*, May 14, 1992.

MONOPOLIES

There was not much succour from the protectors of the public interest, the Monopolies and Mergers Commission (MMC) and the Office of Fair Trading (OFT). When Sir Gordon Borrie retired from the OFT in 1992, after sixteen years as director, he belatedly urged the government to introduce laws to prevent cartels in industry, particularly in banks: 'small businesses do not have a lot of choice when it comes to banking services.' But the government was not prepared to take on the big banks. The major moves against monopolies are in the hands of the MMC, currently chaired by Sir Sydney Lipworth, a South African tax lawyer, but it has been vulnerable to political pressures: after botching their confrontation with the brewers they produced a feeble report on the car market which still allowed companies to buy much more cheaply than individuals.

The British, with their long history of cartels, have always been tolerant of monopolies. The Conservatives are reluctant to confront giant companies which contribute to their funds, while the trades unions in the past have preferred to deal with semi-monopolies, nationalised or private. And the big companies have a wide and shrewd embrace – particularly the brewers. At the annual banquet for the Whitbread Book Award the most important guest may not be the prize-winner but the man from the Department of Trade and Industry who supervises brewers' monopolies.

The ravages of recession have increased the imbalance between big companies and small. Hopes for tougher action against monopolies, like so many other hopes, are moving towards Brussels, where the British Commissioner Sir Leon Brittan has made some reputation as a trust-buster, while the British government thankfully passes the buck to his office. But Brittan has his own problems with pressures on a continental scale; and most of the excessive British concentrations of business power can only be cut back by London.

Britain is an island dominated by big corporations, growing bigger: with a small circle of corporate chiefs at the top. The old version of the corporate state which revolved round nationalised industries and trades unions has been dismantled; but Mrs Thatcher came much closer to top industrialists than any other post-war prime minister. And with all her talk of reviving small business her favourites were a small group of barons who each ruled their own territory – including Lord Laing of Biscuits, Lord King of Airlines, Lord Forte of Hotels, Lord Sterling of P & O, Lord

Young of Cable & Wireless – who made the most of their influence with government to maintain their own power.

The concentration of power has strictly limited the range of choice which was promised with deregulation. The big corporations, increasingly specialised and self-contained, are too preoccupied with short-term profits to think much about wider responsibilities to culture and communities. The uniformity can be seen by any traveller visiting motorway cafés or staying in hotels where the big chains maximise profits by bulk-buying. The varieties of service which are more evident on the continent depend on the enterprise of small businessmen who have suffered more than anyone in Britain. The United States, which inspired so much of British policy in the eighties, now presents its own warnings of how unregulated commercial competition can undermine standards and cultural variety. And the undermining is most clearly seen in the most powerful medium, television.

12

Journalists and the Media

Who are the watchdogs to bark at abuses of power? The most obvious has been the Fourth Estate (the phrase was first used by Fielding in 1752 to describe the mob, but later by Carlyle in 1837 to describe the Press). But new owners have interlinked the media with global financial interests over the last decade. The older Press families, the Harmsworths, Beaverbrooks or Astors, were preoccupied with political influence in Britain and less interested in other businesses. In the seventies most newspapers were making a loss, or a slender profit. The Wapping revolution in the eighties broke union power, released new technology and made newspapers for a time much more profitable. It transferred a billion pounds a year from the printers to the owners and journalists. But the new owners, including Murdoch, Maxwell, Black and Rowland, saw their British newspapers as supporting their global empires.

NATIONAL NEWSPAPERS IN 1981 AND 1991/92

Daily Newspapers	Proprietor	Circulation (1991–2) (Oct–Mar)	Circulation (1981) (July–Dec)
Daily Mirror	ex-Maxwell	3,622,739	3,413,785
Sun	Rupert Murdoch	3,618,835	4,136,927
Daily Mail	Lord Rothermere	1,677,147	1,887,051
Daily Express	Lord Stevens	1,501,447	2,126,248
Daily Telegraph	Conrad Black	1,052,961	1,342,007
Daily Star	Lord Stevens	811,591	1,508,000
Today	Rupert Murdoch	466,631	–
Guardian	Guardian Trust	417,314	397,708
Times	Rupert Murdoch	390,401	297,787
Independent	Newspaper Publishing	371,411	–
Financial Times	Pearson Group	290,691	197,742

Sunday Newspapers	Proprietor	Circulation (1991–2) (Oct–Mar)	Circulation (1981) (July–Dec)
News of the World	Rupert Murdoch	4,734,336	4,236,715
Sunday Mirror	ex-Maxwell	2,810,658	3,786,454

People	ex-Maxwell	2,152,931	3,629,687
Mail on Sunday	Lord Rothermere	2,010,807	–
Sunday Express	Lord Stevens	1,666,993	2,993,763
Sunday Times	Rupert Murdoch	1,173,490	1,363,640
Sunday Telegraph	Conrad Black	560,889	916,644
Observer	Tiny Rowland	550,310	886,985
Independent on Sunday	Newspaper Publishing	377,826	–
Sunday Sport	David Sullivan	343,972	–

Most of the press barons are foreigners who spend much of their time outside Britain. No other western country has such an absentee ownership. Rupert Murdoch moves between Los Angeles and Australia; Lord Rothermere, the great-nephew of the *Daily Mail*'s founder, lives in Paris. Conrad Black is a Canadian, with newspapers in Canada, the United States, Jerusalem and Australia. Tiny Rowland, originally German, has most of his interests in Africa, the Middle East and Mexico, between which he is constantly flying. Global ownership does not necessarily make the newspapers internationalist: when the *Sunday Telegraph* was most chauvinist in the late eighties it had a Canadian proprietor (Conrad Black), a New Zealand chief executive (Andrew Knight) and a half-Belgian editor (Peregrine Worsthorne). Canadian or Australian ownership did not encourage British editors to provide a European perspective and political journalists preferred the familiar dramas of Westminster to the foreign languages and alien systems of Brussels or Bonn.

But the owners naturally want to use their papers to fortify their business empires. The Murdoch Press, led by *The Times* and the *Sun*, dutifully boost their master's Sky Television and attack its main rival, the BBC. Tiny Rowland uses the *Observer* to promote his African interests, and to flatter Qhadaffi before selling him a share of his hotels. The *Telegraph* is encouraged by Conrad Black to be 'correct' in its international alignment, supporting the United States government, the National Party in South Africa or Likud in Israel. Among daily papers only the *Independent* and the *Guardian* are independent of corporate pressures: though the *Financial Times*, still controlled by the Pearson family under its chairman Lord Blakenham, became more daring under a new editor Richard Lambert, who launched investigations and even told readers to vote Labour in April 1992.

In the age of information media power becomes more valuable everywhere. Like railways in the last century it can provide keys to other kingdoms: not just to politics or peerages, but to oilfields, television stations or the rest of the entertainment industry – where fame can make or break fortunes. A master-showman like Richard Branson can use his flair and balloons to promote first a record company, then an airline and now special trains.

As the Press boomed through the eighties, it grew less distinct from other powers. While tabloids came closer to showbiz, most 'posh papers' came closer to politics and business: their journalists became less bohemian and more conformist – they wore dark suits, drank less and sat in front of computer-screens. The nostalgia for the drunken journalist in the play *Jeffrey Bernard is Unwell* was a sign of the sobering up. And the editors accepted knighthoods.

Prosperity has extracted a price. Most newspapers are much more Conservative than their readers or journalists (half of the *Telegraph* journalists are anti-Tory). The bias and stridency of their election propaganda in April 1992 amazed foreign observers: 'it is journalism of a kind now hardly known in the United States,' wrote Anthony Lewis in the *New York Times*: 'grotesquely partisan, shamelessly advancing one party's cause. And almost all of it is pro-Conservative.' When Neil Kinnock blamed the Tory Press for his defeat the *Sun* retorted that the complaint had 'not a word of truth', yet after the election it had boasted 'IT'S THE SUN WOT WON IT'. And Major was quick to thank the editors of the *Sun, Daily Mail* and *Daily Express* – two of them Tory knights – for their support.

The links between newspapers and big business had a longer-term effect: for journalists have been constrained from reporting or criticising the excesses of the financial boom, by pressures from owners, advertisers and public relations men, who helped set the agenda of the business pages. Entrepreneurial owners naturally dislike the critical and investigative function of reporters. But the Press is important for business battles, and take-overs and mergers provided trials of strength for the rival public relations men to push shares through their friendships with journalists. When Lord Hanson bid for ICI he was faced with a salvo of newspaper stories about his horse-racing colleague Lord White, and blamed his public relations adviser Sir Tim Bell, rather than the editors, for his bad press.

The libel lawyers could quell criticism of buccaneers, even crooks. The Maxwell scandal embarrassed more than anyone the journalists, including this one, who could not reveal beforehand that he was a crook. And the media could not deploy an effective countervailing force to the financial concentrations of the eighties. It was left to the satirical fortnightly *Private*

Eye, which dared to risk libel, to be the scourge of racketeers from Maxwell to BCCI.

Britain has eleven national daily papers, not including the *Sporting Life* and the *Racing Post*, and the publicans' *Morning Advertiser*: more than any other western country, and much more centralised on one city than papers in the United States, Germany or France. They include some of the best and the worst in the world, and they appear to offer a wide freedom of choice, all the way from the *Financial Times* down to the *Sun* – still lower on Sundays, to the sex-fantasies of the *Sunday Sport*. Yet they have growing limitations – even the five 'quality papers' – as representatives of their readers' interests. They compete increasingly for short-term news, rather than longer-term analysis or reflection; and their short horizons make them still more vulnerable to the government's news-management, photo opportunities, briefings or leaks. They are all – even the *Guardian* which came from Manchester – preoccupied with London, fascinated by each other, living in a bright-lit hall of mirrors, cut off from the dingier provinces and suburbs. They become more preoccupied by parliament and opinion polls rather than their own reports of political grass-roots. They all lack investigative reporting, whether about the unemployed, racial minorities, provincial politics or the groundswells of public discontent. They all project a life-style of hectic spending and travelling, heavily influenced by advertisers, and play down non-commercial tastes, whether for poetry, old books or the countryside.

Foreign ownership released the Press from traditional restraints. Rupert Murdoch who controls 33 per cent of the British Press has seen himself as shaking up the class-bound British establishment, and breaking tribal taboos: he has confused quality with snobbery, and taken his more prestigious papers downmarket. The *Sunday Times*, determined to challenge the *Mail on Sunday*, serialised first the marital problems of the Princess of Wales and then Goebbels' diaries. Murdoch offered the editorship of *The Times* to a man who preferred to edit the *Daily Mail*. Both moves obscured the distinction between entertainment and information.

Press power was becoming cruder, more like the old days of Hearst (Citizen Kane) in America, as owners and editors collected sexual secrets and waited to reveal them, a tactic which verged on blackmail and effectively intimidated politicians. The players were not interested in checking abuses of power, but in joining in the power-game, and extending their own share.

TELEVISION

Television has greater scope and resources for investigating and revealing the misdeeds of government and big business, and it can have much more impact, presenting personalities and events directly to the public with much more credibility than newsprint. British television can show an impressive record of independence and exposure – whether of miscarriages of justice, maltreatment in institutions, or abuses of power by government – and a sharpness of satire, as in *Spitting Image*, which can amaze Americans. The alternative channels, BBC2 and Channel 4, have deliberately catered for creative and uncommercial minorities, providing a wider range of outlook than the Press. And British television is still regarded by many foreigners as the best in the world.

But television is constantly vulnerable both to commercial pressures and to pressures from government, which is always much more criticised than the opposition, since it makes the key decisions; and the longer a government is in power, the more it forgets television's benefits in opposition. The Conservatives receive more effective criticism from television than from the Press, and many of them look to more competition to weaken the power of the television controllers.

And free competition can easily demoralise the confidence of the programmers. For television plays out on the screen the dilemma which runs through so many areas of British life including schools, hospitals and universities: how to compete more vigorously while safeguarding high standards. And this dilemma threatens the whole identity of the BBC as the traditional guardian of public service broadcasting.

The centralised power of the BBC has been under fire since the fifties, when it was first challenged by commercial television in 1956. It came under more bombardment in 1974 when Roy Jenkins appointed Lord Annan to head a Committee on the future of broadcasting, which criticised its 'institutional malaise' and unitary control. But the BBC went on growing, overmanned and centralised, a fat sitting duck; and in it Mrs Thatcher diagnosed what she most disliked – leftist paternalism, purveyed by south-eastern intellectuals with foreign names. Beeb people were certainly vulnerable, cut off behind their own canteens, office politics and team-travel: they preferred to see and interview each other, and disliked dialogues with the viewers. 'I've got fifty advisory committees,' one Director-General boasted to me, 'and I take no notice of any of them.'

They became more cut off under their first home-grown Director-General Alasdair Milne, a clever Wykehamist who lacked the political antennae to sense danger. Mrs Thatcher appointed an urbane new chairman Marmaduke Hussey, who swiftly despatched Milne and replaced him with his accountant deputy Michael Checkland, more careful in avoiding controversy and controlling costs. And more power rested with the governors, an odd mix of academics and administrators, including an obligatory diplomat and trade unionist.

BBC GOVERNORS IN APRIL 1992

	Background
Marmaduke Hussey, chairman	ex-chief executive, *The Times*
Lord Barnett, vice-chairman	ex-Labour cabinet minister
Sir Kenneth Bloomfield	Head of N.I. Civil Service
Jane Glover	conductor of London Mozart Players
Sir Graham Hills	Vice-Chancellor, Strathclyde University
Lady James	thriller writer, ex-civil servant; Tory life peer
Dr Gwyn Jones	software businessman, North Wales
Bill Jordan	President, Amalgamated Engineering Union
Lord Nicholas Gordon Lennox	ex-Ambassador
Keith Oates	finance director, Marks and Spencer
Dr John Roberts	historian, Oxford
Mrs Shahwar Sadeque	physicist; Conservative activist, from Bangladesh.

The new director in 1992, John Birt, was already a power inside the BBC: an austere presence, with intense eyes and close-cropped hair; trained as an engineer, not an accountant. He came to television from Liverpool and Oxford and later proclaimed with his friend Peter Jay his 'mission to explain'. He certainly shows a sense of purpose in current affairs. But the BBC still faces continuing insecurity as it prepares for the renewal of the licence fee in 1996: still with a staff of 25,000 even after sub-contracting programmes to small companies. 'The BBC bureaucracy looks increasingly isolated,' complained their new paymaster, the Minister of Arts David Mellor, 'in a world where most other management organisations have moved from that kind of bureaucracy.'

The BBC, as it awaits its new charter and licence fee in 1996, is caught between two roles. It still sees itself as a central part of the constitution, committed to high standards. 'Without the BBC,' says their correspondent John Simpson, 'we would be a less united kingdom. It has given us shared notions of who we are, what we are concerned with, what we find funny.'

But it is assailed by commercial networks, satellites and cables which can claim to be closer to popular taste.

INDEPENDENT TELEVISION

Commercial television has undergone deeper changes. The original Television Act of 1954 established a powerful regulating body, the Independent Broadcasting Authority (IBA), which awarded franchises to the most acceptable contractors and insisted on a proportion of quality programmes: a system deliberately designed to avoid American vices. It was a form of public service television financed by advertising. This kind of paternalism annoyed Mrs Thatcher, and the commercial stations were politically vulnerable, absurdly overmanned and exploited by the unions. She was exasperated by television investigations, particularly by Thames Television's exposure of the government's ruthless counter-terrorism in Gibraltar in *Death on the Rock* which had been approved by the IBA's chairman Lord Thomson. Mrs Thatcher was resolved to shake up the existing television companies and to reduce regulation, and created a new body, the Independent Television Commission (ITC), which had less control over schedules: it would award contracts primarily on the basis of tenders, like building contractors, producing more revenues for the Treasury.

In the resulting auction Thames Television, the biggest London station, lost its franchise to Carlton Television under Michael Green. The breakfast station TV AM, run by Mrs Thatcher's friend Greg Dyke, had upgraded its news programmes after a warning by the IBA; now it lost its franchise to a higher bidder who would economise with the costs of news.

MAJOR TELEVISION COMPANIES IN 1992

Company	Chairman	Background
Anglia	Sir Peter Gibbings	ex-*Guardian* chairman
Border	James Graham	BBC Editor
Central	Leslie Hill	EMI director; accountant
Channel	John Riley	Jersey senator; Guards
Grampian	Sir Douglas Hardie	businessman
Granada	Charles Allen	caterer
HTV	Louis Sherwood	Gateway supermarkets
LWT	Brian Tesler	television producer
Scottish	William Brown	television salesman

Tyne Tees	Sir Ralph Carr-Ellison	Lord Lieutenant
Ulster	John McGuckian	businessman
Yorkshire	Sir Derek Palmar	businessman
Channel 4	Sir Richard Attenborough	film director

From January 1993 four new licence holders:

Company	Chairman	Background
Carlton	Michael Green	television executive; son-in-law of Lord Wolfson
Good Morning	Harry Roach	chairman, *Guardian*
Meridian	Roger Laughton	BBC executive
West Country	Steven Redfarne	banker

The new competitiveness made all the companies feel less secure, and more preoccupied with short-term profits. The last prestigious drama series produced by Thames Television, *Anglo-Saxon Attitudes*, cost £700,000 an hour, which was hard to justify without the need to impress the IBA. Granada fired their television chairman David Plowright who had commissioned their high-quality drama, and turned further towards crime shows. Deregulation has also threatened the diversity which was inherent in the earlier system which required companies to be identified with the locality in which they were based: when they bid for their franchises they had to look as regional as possible, putting local grandees and businessmen on their boards and local heroes on their programmes. A few lived up to their promises: Granada Television has convincingly projected Lancashire as Granadaland. But networked programmes and American dramas offer much cheaper schedules, and more conformity. The new chief executive of Independent Television, Andrew Quinn, has warned that there will be more mergers between regional companies in the next years, while insisting that 'ITV's regional character can be preserved regardless of ownership'. But Quinn has emphasised his preoccupation with ratings as opposed to cultural or crusading aims. Current affairs programmes, he says, can be made to get people out of prison provided that at least eight million people want to watch them.[1]

Even commercial radio has become less local. Stations which began by purveying their news and culture, with home-town journalists investigating local scandals and interviewing mayors, soon found pop music much cheaper and less liable to switch-off, particularly during 'drive-time'; and

[1] *The Times*, August 4, 1992.

the recession saw big cut-backs in local staffing. Radio listening in Britain has gone up rapidly, from eight to ten hours a week in the four years to 1990, while television viewing has gone down, from twenty-six to twenty-four hours a week – partly because of competition with videos.[2] But more competition has threatened the highbrow programmes, including BBC Radio 3 which now broadcasts less music, and more chat.

But the real underminers of any national television system are the satellites and cables which can bring international programmes to growing numbers of viewers. Within the next years the richest television company is likely to be BSkyB, controlled by Rupert Murdoch, which has been multiplying its viewers by acquiring monopolies for televising sports: first the Cricket World Cup, and then Premier League football, for which it paid £304 million, with the help of the BBC in May 1992. The high cost of programmes inevitably makes television more dependent on the world market place, and the British companies themselves will eventually be open to non-British bidders which can make them part of global empires. The European television barons, like the Italian Berlusconi or André Rousselet who controls Canal Plus in France, have much bigger resources than the British companies, which may themselves have to merge with each other to compete. A few 'Sky Barons' will be competing across the world, and the contest to control global news, initiated by CNN, will raise the stakes further. Once again the future leads to Europe.

The new technologies will enable viewers to subscribe to specially desirable programmes, like sporting events or porn films, to produce a more fragmented market. The film producer David Puttnam estimates that by the end of the century the average viewer will be spending the equivalent of £500 a year in today's money on audio-visual programmes; and reckons that this fragmentation will increase class divisions. For the better-educated viewers will prefer the more sophisticated and compulsive pleasures of interactive television which can provide the equivalent of encyclopaedias on the screen, extending their cultural and historical knowledge – distinguishing them still more thoroughly than book reading or theatre-going from the rest of the population who will depend on mass-programmes.

Forty years after commercial television was first mooted in Britain deregulation and competition have brought it closer to the American

[2] *Social Trends*, 1992, p. 177–8.

patterns its founders sought to avoid. The extreme free-marketeers in Britain, led by the Murdoch interests, present the intensified competition as a victory for democracy, which will give viewers maximum choice. But American television shows how illusory that choice can become, so that most intelligent Americans ignore television altogether. In Britain the earlier idealism of television as an educational and cultural medium has evaporated in the perpetual anxiety about ratings; and the 'electronic village' of the sixties, in which the whole nation would watch *Panorama* together, has fragmented into class divisions like newspapers and magazines which do not try to bridge the gap. As Alan Bennett puts it:

> The very same people who fuss about the nation losing its identity in Europe are quite happy to see national television lose its identity and go the European way, so that we end up with a diet of pap and crap. One wants to ask such people: what is it that helps to hold the nation together? A shared interest in the novels of Lord Archer?[3]

The BBC becomes still more confused about its role, together with many other public broadcasting systems which it inspired around the world. As it looks ahead to the renewal of its charter and licence fee, it feels more impelled to compete for mass-viewers and to reach downmarket without real conviction: in the summer of 1992 it launched a half-baked soap opera *Eldorado* which showed all its lack of confidence. Yet it can only justify its licence fee if it provides a genuinely alternative service with high standards – which becomes more needed as commercial television becomes more conformist, and the government more demanding. Unfortunately the BBC's self-containment cuts it off from audiences who could be its main support: its main feedback on the screen consists in reading out comments from viewers in funny voices, and it takes little notice of the well-organised lobby for maintaining broadcast standards, Voice of Listener and Viewer (VLV). As one member of VLV complained: 'We must save the BBC from itself.'

The insecurity and short-termness of the media strictly limit their ability to widen British horizons. The earlier hopes that television would provide an unprecedented means of national education have long faded; and it

---

[3] *A Night with Alan Bennett*, BBC2, July 5, 1992.

has never realised its potential as a purveyor of culture and history – though the Open University has shown the way.

More serious is the inability of the Press and television in the political field, to counterbalance a continuing party in power – which most newspaper proprietors have no wish to do anyway. The shorter their horizons, the more all the media are limited to the agenda and assumptions set by the government, and the less they can stand back and take a longer and wider view of Britain in the setting of Europe or the whole world. And the less they are inclined to represent the grievances or aspirations of the unrepresented, outside the narrow circles of Westminster and Whitehall.

13

Workers and Workless

In the faded Victorian ballroom of the Winter Gardens in Blackpool, the Trades Union Congress met for their 124th Annual Conference in September 1992 in a much more subdued mood. The year before they had looked forward to a return of the Labour Party which they had first brought into being to protect their interests: now they were landed with another four Tory years. In their chastened mood they had even for the first time in their history invited the employers' leader – the director of the Confederation of British Industry, Howard Davies. When he got up to speak the miners' leader Arthur Scargill made one of his traditional exits; and Roger Lyons, the leader of the scientific and financial union, later attacked the CBI as the 'willing and craven accomplice' of the Tories. But most members approved of opening a dialogue with the employers, and welcomed Davies' offer to keep his door open.

The unions' moderation was not surprising; for they now represented only a third of Britain's workforce, and the membership of nearly all the big unions had shrunk. At this conference their main theme was the need for more jobs: the banner above the platform dais proclaimed 'WORKING FOR FULL EMPLOYMENT' and the speeches were full of stories of mass-firings and low wages. Garfield Davies, the head of the shop-workers' union USDAW, quoted wages as low as £1.40 an hour for a railway guard in Newcastle, and £1.80 for a cleaner in Glasgow. But the TUC had been powerless either to prevent a new surge of unemployment, or to achieve what all other workers in Europe could rely on: a minimum wage. The TUC conference had always been more than a meeting of bargaining forces: it had been the bark of the underdog. And now that bark was almost silenced.

The atmosphere was hardly recognisable compared to the TUC conference I had watched thirty years earlier. Then it was a kind of proletarian rally, with rows of rugged, angry-looking men in braces, open-necks and heavy shoes, and leaders on the platform who looked ready for physical fights: like the ex-lorry driver Frank Cousins, or the boilermaker Ted Hill who referred to all bosses as rascals. They bellowed their speeches as if they were on the parade ground, and could intimidate the Labour politicians, personnel officers and industrial camp-followers who came up to Black-pool, anxiously to observe the strike leaders who could hold industries to ransom.

Now in 1992 the ballroom was full of brightly-dressed women, well-groomed bank clerks or sober tax inspectors alongside the factory-workers. The speakers were more articulate and brisk than at many business conferences, with a striking mixture of classes, and every kind of accent from Gorbals to Roedean. Most of them talked not to comrades but to brothers and sisters, and one bank employee even quoted Aeschylus who 'as we know' said in *Agamemnon* that 'the people's voice is a mighty force'. Nearly everyone was making references to the European Community: usually not arguing for or against it, but how to use it, adapt it and democratise it. One stall offered the TUC's 'European Information Service'; another was launching an Anglo-German campaign for a Europe-wide debate on the right to work, and an English version of the German unions' monthly *Mitbestim-mung*. The TUC Council had just committed itself to develop alliances through a new 'Network Europe' and to 'bridge the gap between developments in Brussels and the everyday work of trades unionists in Britain'.

It was a wide gap to bridge; for within Britain the division between top and bottom had become much greater in the eighties. It was part of a greater inequality all through the West, speeded up by the more intensive world competition and new technologies, which had left unqualified workers further behind. But in Britain the gap was widened by the concentration of power at the centre and the weakened representation at the circumference. The glare of publicity and attention was spotlighted on the small cast of characters, while the spokesmen for the rest of the population had disappeared out of sight.

THE UNIONS' DECLINE

The most spectacular disappearing-act has come from the trades-unions leaders, most of all at election time. 'I am the ghost of elections past,' joked Tom Sawyer, the Deputy-Secretary of NUPE and chairman of the

Labour Party, at Neil Kinnock's silver wedding a month before the 1992 election: 'I am a trade union official.'

Through the sixties and seventies the trades unions were still regarded by all parties as part of the constitution, 'the Fifth Estate' coming after the Commons and the Press. Ted Heath had said, 'The trouble is not that the trades unions are too strong. They are too weak.' Successive prime ministers cultivated the union leaders; and at the peak were the 'gold-plated six' who helped to plan Britain's industrial future with businessmen and ministers in Neddy. The governments' respect for trades unionists was partly based on fear; Conservatives were inclined to see them as sergeant-majors controlling troops who were potentially mutinous but indispensable; while Labour ministers were conscious of their financial dependence, and the class gap. Both parties shied away from confrontation.

Mrs Thatcher had no such fear. She began by simply refusing to talk to the union leaders – 'no beer and sandwiches at Number Ten' – who suddenly seemed more like ordinary men, as if the arc-lights had been switched off. And soon their unions were seriously weakened by the surge of unemployment which lost them half a million members in a year.

They first saw it as a passing phase. 'When this Conservative administration is long forgotten,' Rodney Bickerstaffe, the champion of low-paid workers in NUPE assured me, 'the British trade union movement will still be going strong. The flame will not die. Even with a totally hostile government and six or seven acts of parliament, trades unions are still there.' But it proved a very long phase. After the 1983 election the Secretary of the TUC Len Murray tried to advocate a 'new realism', which could lead to collaboration with government; but after meeting Mrs Thatcher he said: 'we're in two different worlds.' Soon afterwards he retired early.

The big unions still exerted their influence over the Labour Party which they had first invented. When Michael Foot resigned they were behind the choice of Neil Kinnock as leader. But they had themselves damaged the Labour Party's prospects, by associating it with the mythology of the Winter of Discontent, with the mounting strikes and wage-claims, the neglected hospitals, the uncollected rubbish, the unburied dead, which had provided the Tories with all the ammunition they needed.

TUC – TOP 10 UNIONS 1992

Union	Membership (000s)		Head
	1992	1982	
Transport and General			
Workers' (TGWU)	1,223	1,692	Bill Morris
General, Municipal and			
Boilermakers' (GMB)	933	866	John Edmonds
National and Local Government			
Officers' Association (NALGO)	744	796	Alan Jinkinson
Amalgamated Engineering			
Union (AEUW)	702	1,104	Gavin Laird
Manufacturing, Science and			
Finance (MSF)	653	428	Ken Gill
National Union of Public			
Employees (NUPE)	579	704	Rodney Bickerstaffe
Union of Shop, Distributive and			
Allied Workers (USDAW)	361	438	Garfield Davies
Graphical, Paper and			
Media Union (GPMU)	288	–	Tony Dubbins
Union of Construction, Allied			
Trades and Technicians (UCATT)	207	275	Albert Williams
Confederation of Health			
Service Employees (COHSE)	203	–	Hector Mackenzie

Mrs Thatcher was now free to break union power, with successive legislation and showdowns, culminating in the long miners' strike and the defeat of Arthur Scargill – which finally undermined the fear and guilt that the miners had evoked ever since their strike in 1926. Today the public no longer sees the unions as any kind of estate. The government feels no need to woo them, and the Minister for Employment has very limited contact with union leaders. Trades union members have gone down from 12½ to 8¼ million, while total employment has remained roughly level. Most of the new jobs are casual, part-time, low-paid, and non-unionised; and the new workers are more fearful of losing their jobs.

Yet attitudes to work seem little affected. As Robert Worcester of MORI puts it: 'Britain's working population has doggedly sat through the whole experience – through the wildly different prime ministerships of James Callaghan and Margaret Thatcher – and emerged at the other end with their attitudes to work almost entirely unmoved and unchanged. In 1989 82 per cent of workers were either very satisfied, or fairly satisfied, with their jobs, according to MORI, compared to 83 per cent in 1976. But in

[137]

spite of the more hostile atmosphere to unions, in 1989 58 per cent of workers still agreed that 'trades unions are essential to protect workers' interests'.[1]

The big unions have all lost members. In March 1992 a Jamaican chief executive, Bill Morris, took over the biggest union, the Transport and General Workers' (TGWU) with a staff of a thousand and 1.2 million members. But the membership has shrunk by a half since 1979, and Morris could make much less impact than earlier giants, like Jack Jones in the seventies or Frank Cousins in the sixties – let alone Ernest Bevin in the thirties. All the bigger unions are now trying to merge into 'super-unions' to compensate for dwindling membership. The TGWU may eventually combine with the miners' union, without Arthur Scargill; while the engineers' AEU is planning to merge with the electricians' EETPU, which could then attract the MSF (Manufacturing, Science and Finance). The three public-sector unions, NUPE, NALGO and COHSE, are planning to create the biggest of all. They were once seen as the terrible trio, blamed for the Winter of Discontent in 1979: but now their merger raises few fears. The three super-unions would become financially more viable, and together would account for half the membership of the TUC; but they would limit its role. 'If that happens,' Norman Willis has said, 'I'm out of a job.'

The dread of union power and strikes now belongs to a remote earlier era: of endless daily headlines about strikes, television interviews at factory gates and last-minute dramas of deadlock and conciliation. Negotiators, labour correspondents and personnel officers all now seem less important. No change wrought by Mrs Thatcher was more fundamental than the cutting-down of unions – which brought their leaders' relations with industrialists much closer to the continental pattern.

Their future prospects of regaining influence still depend heavily on the return of the Labour Party, which they still finance. John Smith and many of his shadow cabinet would like to loosen their links and find alternative backers, for they blame the unions for their defeat in 1979 and their failures since. They cannot, however, forget their obligations to the unions: all of the shadow cabinet are affiliated to a union (see page 29), six of them to the TGWU, five to GMT, and they will remain dependent on

[1] Eric Jacobs and Robert Worcester: *We British*, Weidenfeld & Nicholson, London, 1990, pp. 114–15.

the unions for the foreseeable future. But they have little desire to reinstate the Fifth Estate.

The union leaders in the meantime look outside Britain for much of their future strengthening. The TUC is now more European-minded than the cabinet and their General Secretary, Norman Willis, currently President of the European TUC, is committed to close links with the Community. The move towards Europe was boosted in 1988 when Jacques Delors addressed the TUC Congress. As Willis described the conversion to me in March 1992:

> It became clear in the mid eighties that people were doing creative work in the European Community, and social policy was becoming stronger. Our position on Europe had become detached from reality, and we had the good judgment or good luck to invite Delors. I saw much evidence in Europe that the social partnership is part of the economic success.
>
> We realised that we must not just put up with the European Community, but make the best of it. And we got a response from the Community which was totally lacking from the government. We found a home in a Social Europe, not just on the rebound, but in a positive sense. Now I believe that we have a responsibility to show that European democracies can deliver the goods economically.

The widening of the unions' horizons may eventually prove as significant as their humiliation by Thatcher; and many union leaders have been converted to working with their counterparts in the Community – and elsewhere in the industrial world. Ron Todd when he was General Secretary of the TGWU in 1988 told the annual Congress: 'The only card game in town at the moment is in a town called Brussels. We've got to learn the rules, and pretty fast.' The worldly Deputy-Secretary of the TUC, David Lea, is a tireless attender of international conferences, well-informed about multinationals and Japanese industry. Gavin Laird, the Glaswegian Secretary of the engineers' union, is a strong advocate of Japanese investment in Britain, and angrily attacked the 'crass stupidity' of the TUC Council when they condemned Japanese working practices. Rodney Bickerstaffe of NUPE, the champion of low-paid workers, is now a convinced European. 'Europe is looking to Britain to join the Social Charter, and a European TUC adds to our horizons.' He looks to the world trades unions to control the multinationals, the 'giants who stride across the borders'. And he insists that unions will 'have a real and vital role at every level, domestic, European and international'.

Within Britain, in the meantime, the weakness of the unions presents dangers as well as benefits. Both governments and employers will still need their workers' support for any long-term plans to modernise and expand industry, or to implement the training programmes which are essential for Britain to compete with Europe and Japan. And the undermining of the unions upsets the balance between labour and capital: even in America George Shultz, the Republican former secretary of the Treasury, has warned that unions should be stronger, for the sake of a healthy society.

And the unions' loss of influence has left a huge gap in representation, not just at the work-place, but in wide areas of Britain where people have been left behind, too unorganised or low-paid to influence government in London. The annual Congress was always more than a show of strength by a bargaining force. It was the opportunity for all kinds of neglected groups, whether at home or abroad, to find a voice. It was the bark of the underdog – now almost silenced. Once people lose their job, they lose their union, and the TUC inevitably loses interest in them. The unemployed have nobody to speak for them in what they call 'the dolers' union'.

UNEMPLOYED

No political attitudes have changed more drastically over thirty years than attitudes towards unemployment. After the Second World War both parties regarded the maintaining of full employment as a prime responsibility of government; the Treaty of Rome in 1957 committed members in Article 104 to 'ensuring a high level of employment'. When economists like Professor Frank Paish at the London School of Economics first began to say in the late fifties that higher unemployment was the inevitable price of economic efficiency they were regarded as heretics. When unemployment started rising rapidly in the seventies many Labour leaders expected trouble. Then, under Thatcher in the early eighties, unemployment rose to undreamt-of levels, to two million, and under Nigel Lawson to over three million – for the first time since 1933. At each new jump Len Murray of the TUC expected riots in the streets. But the areas of high unemployment showed a ghostly silence; and the few reporters who visited them were surprised to find apathy rather than anger. Unemployment fell during the late eighties but by September 1992 it was up again to 9.7 per cent, much higher than in Germany, America or Japan, though less than France or Italy. There is now much less talk of intolerable levels and thoughts of revolution. Both government and opposition leaders accept high unemployment as a fact of economic life; while the jobless still do not make themselves heard.

There are some obvious reasons. Many unemployed are in constituencies with large Labour majorities whose members of parliament do not need to woo their vote, and know they have no other party to vote for. Many are too disorganised or unrooted to form any lobby or group. Some are working in the black economy to supplement the dole with cash jobs which never reach the statistics.

But the central fact is that Britain's system of representation revolves round organised jobs; and those without jobs have no framework within which to organise. Over the years they accept that they are never likely to have a job; and they and their families become part of a culture of unemployment. They are not an underclass on the American scale; and Mrs Thatcher dismisses the word itself as a Marxist fallacy. But the British are beginning to have a group of people, like the American underclass, who feel permanently cut off by race and background from the industrial system. Unlike the earlier British underclass at the beginning of the century, they are protected by the dole: but when they look for a job they face higher walls, and a much more organised and disciplined system. Only government action is likely to provide them with the ladders.

The great majority of British have seen a higher material standard of living over twenty years. In 1971 9 per cent of households had no access to a bathroom or shower; in 1990 only 1 per cent. In 1971 65 per cent of households still had no central heating; in 1990 only 22 per cent. Household spending on food fell between 1976 and 1990, from 19.2 per cent of total spending to 12.7 per cent, while transport and communications had gone up from 15.4 per cent to 18.4 per cent. Luxuries of one decade had become the necessities of the next. 80 per cent of households now have deep-freezes, 86 per cent washing machines, 87 per cent telephones, 93 per cent colour televisions. 60 per cent have video-recorders, and 47 per cent have microwave ovens. For those in work, holidays have become more generous: in 1990 nine out of ten full-time manual workers were entitled to more than four weeks' paid holiday a year: twenty years ago only two-thirds were allowed three weeks or more. And foreign holidays were commonplace: household expenditure abroad had more than trebled (at constant prices) in the fifteen years to 1990. But the contrast is all the more acute with the have-nots, and particularly with immigrants. And those at the bottom face above all a shortage of space: only 1 per cent of total households have less than one room per person, but among non-whites the proportion is 10 per cent and among Pakistanis or Bangladeshis 33 per cent.[2]

In the late eighties the numbers of homeless surged, until by 1990 local authorities accepted that half a million people were officially homeless and entitled to housing – not including single people or couples without children. The recession, the shortage of council-houses and the lack of care for the mentally ill had all swollen the numbers, and the homeless were having to look to churches and charities: as the Bishop of Salisbury warned in July 1992, 'we are moving in an era when Government will no longer pick up so much of the tab for human need.'

It was the underside of the boom of the eighties: in London, as in New York and Paris, the homeless are sleeping in city streets and parks for the first time since before the Second World War. Any visitor can see the scenes of contrast, like the campers on makeshift beds with cardboard shelters sleeping among the dripping bushes of Lincoln's Inn Fields, just outside the comfortable heartland of the lawyers. The cutbacks on Welfare in the eighties, and the limitations of local government, have reduced the provision for outcasts, including families who cannot pay their rent, young people thrown out by their parents or new immigrants with no one to look after them. Some are given the crudest kind of temporary accommodation, including bed and breakfast hotels which provide wretched conditions for children. Others sleep rough and make their homes in subways, under railway-bridges or in square gardens.

The homeless have little access to politicians or the media, with a few exceptions like their lively fortnightly *The Big Issue* which they themselves sell in the streets. It gives some insight into the scale of the problem: the 250,000 who are estimated to be missing, the 770,000 dwellings which remain empty while 500,000 people are homeless. Central government does not wish to accept this responsibility: they pass it on to local councils which they themselves have cut back.

[2] *Social Trends*, 1992.

THE OTHER SOCIETY

There are also tens of thousands of families who have voluntarily chosen to escape from the constraints of urban life, to take to the road and spend their lives in tents, caravans or squats. They present a more fundamental challenge to government: for they ask for the right to belong to an alternative society with its own values and priorities, rejecting material achievements and taking pride in their self-sufficiency and closeness to nature – a right which is harder to deny when the conventional society cannot offer them likely employment. They throw an interesting sidelight on the system they have rejected.

They belong to an old romantic tradition, linked to the gypsies who first came to Europe from India in the sixteenth century with a life-style which Cervantes described in 1614: 'We are the Lords of the Universe, of fields, fruits, crops, forests, mountains, of the rivers and springs, of the stars and all the elements.' The British fascination with gypsies was revived at the end the nineteenth century, in a reaction against the growing conformity of city life; and artists, writers and philologists idealised the mysterious Romani people who defied industrial discipline (my grandfather compiled the first dictionary of their language). After two world wars authentic gypsies with their caravans were much rarer, but young British families adopted the romance, dropping out of the towns and driving off in old cars hauling caravans. Today the 'travellers' have very mixed origins and motives, including the New Age travellers who bring their own mysticism and astrology; and their gatherings are sometimes disrupted by 'ravers', drug-takers and disco-dancers. But they are all determined to escape from the cities, and while they live off the dole they expect nothing else from governments except freedom of movement.

But freedom has become harder to find. Local councils, pressed by landowners, have continually tried to stop gypsies or travellers from settling. After angry police battles in the sixties the Labour government passed a Caravan Sites Act in 1968 which required local councils to provide fields for gypsies, while allowing them to eject them from unauthorised places; but councils were slow to provide sites. Travellers too have become more constricted, and the infiltration of violent and druggy groups provoked a new wave of hostility towards all travellers; and in 1992 the government was preparing a White Paper to reduce the councils' obligations. Both gypsies and travellers are more hedged in by officialdom which cannot offer them jobs in the towns, but is intolerant and fearful of their freedom in the country. And while they keep their own pride in their hardiness and tolerance, they feel subjected to the values of an increasingly conformist industrial society.

The treatment of gypsies has often been seen as a pointer to the broader tolerance of nations; and they now face the brunt of the growing intolerance of strangers throughout most of Europe, particularly in Eastern Europe where the great majority live. They have always aroused dark fears because they questioned the fixed rules of communities. Like the Jews they were exiled through the West, keeping their own self-contained culture; but they never sought a homeland, and built up no capital: their families traditionally burnt their belongings when they died. Both Hitler and Stalin tried to get rid of the gypsies, who still managed to survive; but the end of the Cold War presents a new kind of threat, disguised as a blessing. They can cross the Iron Curtain and will soon be able theoretically to move freely through Western Europe: as natural nomads they should be the chief beneficiaries of the opening of frontiers in January 1993. But recession and insecurity has made them feared more than ever, both in the East and the West; and the migration of Roumanian and other gypsies into Germany has provoked ugly riots and right-wing reactions, as they come up against communities with their own insecurities and high unemployment.

The gypsies are only the most exotic part of the wave of immigrants who are moving from Eastern to Western Europe since the end of the Cold War, often creating acute social problems and political backlashes where they try to settle – particularly in Germany which is on the front line and which in the past has been most hospitable to asylum-seekers. The British will still try to restrict immigrants more firmly than the rest of the western continent; but they have all the more obligation to deal tolerantly with those who are already inside their island.

14

Cities and Regions

The proud city halls and municipal centres of Britain symbolise a vanished and self-confident age: the Manchester Free Trade Hall, Leeds Town Hall, the St George's Hall in Liverpool all conjure up a history of civic pride and political independence; while old squares and terraces have been pulled down to provide shopping malls or supermarkets which sell identical products by the same methods across the country. And opposite the Houses of Parliament in Westminster is the most powerful symbol of all, the long façade of County Hall which used to accommodate 6,000 people and has stood empty since 1986 as a ghostly reminder that London once had its own government. Among all the movements towards centralised power the most fundamental has been the undermining of local and regional powers which once were the most effective balances against the centre.

The decline of provincial power has long historical roots, but it has been speeded up over the post-war decades by the centralisation of both government and private finance. The voices of Birmingham, Manchester or Newcastle have become far less audible, as financial and industrial headquarters have moved south. Few people can now remember when great engineering companies were run from the Midlands, or Martin's Bank helped to finance Liverpool, before Barclays swallowed it, almost without trace. The Victorian traditions of provincial leadership, by industrialists like the Chamberlains of Birmingham, landowners like the Derbys of Merseyside, or bankers like the Quaker families of Norfolk, were all undermined by centralisation in London; and only a few members of parliament are now closely identified with the city or region that they represent.

The centralising process has been exacerbated by the London-based media which are more concentrated on the capital than in any major western country. The *Guardian* has lost its Mancunian accent and even Granada Television, the pride of the north, is ultimately controlled by the Granada Group in London. The media reflect the weakness of regional political pressure which is more striking now that London is as depressed

[145]

as many other centres. Cities like Birmingham or Liverpool are determined to assert their own cultural identity, while Manchester is bidding for the Olympics. Glasgow, the European City of Culture for 1990, proudly displayed the creativity of its own school of writers, painters and directors, and in that year it had three million visitors, four times as many as during the mid eighties. But none of them made much impact on London's political monopoly.

Even during general election campaigns the regions have less showing in the national media than thirty years ago, as newspapers rely more on opinion polls, less on local reporting. In the American election year the long-drawn-out pageant of the primaries compels both candidates and reporters to study and record the wide differences between New Hampshire, Texas or California. But in Britain the central drama remains based on daily press conferences in London, or on plane journeys where reporters stay close to the party leaders as they provide carefully-staged photo opportunities for the national media; and political commentators rarely venture north of the Watford Gap.

LOCAL GOVERNMENT

But the most evident change has been in the demoralisation of local government, which has a longer history than national government: in the Middle Ages the county courts made up of freemen of the shire provided the only government that most people knew. But parliament increased its hold, and local councils had no separate constitutional powers, like the French, which were independent of the capital. As councils depended more on central government for their revenues, their independent status was eroded. Class divisions further weakened local councillors: while the old honorific Lord Lieutenants of the counties were toffs, the elected councillors were seen as inferior to metropolitan or imperial administrators. By the sixties governments increasingly interfered with ancient local structures, boundaries and even names; in 1972 the Conservatives pushed through the Local Government Act which drastically redrew the lines of 124 counties and boroughs and over a thousand district councils to produce fewer and bigger counties which have never quite recovered their sense of identity. They abolished Rutland and Cumberland and created new units with names like Avon, Cleveland and Lothian which are still not understood twenty years later.

The next Conservative government caused a much greater upheaval. The big-city councils were already vulnerable, and urgently needed reform: the apathy of voters had allowed them to abuse their power. But Mrs Thatcher was determined to confront these 'last vestiges of feudal power'. She abolished altogether the six metropolitan borough councils, and found in the Greater London Council her arch-enemy. The Greater London Council had actually been created in 1963 by the Tories, who enlarged the Labour-controlled London County Council to include more Conservative boroughs. But when Ken Livingstone captured it as Leader in 1981 he set it on a collision-course with Mrs Thatcher, turning it into a provocative mouthpiece for the Labour Left. The Tories were able to abolish it in 1986 without much public distress; but with the end of the Greater London Council the whole tradition and focus of London government collapsed.

Labour councils had overborrowed and overspent, which gave Mrs Thatcher the chance to move further, and to impose her poll tax, theoretically to make councils more accountable. When it proved her undoing John Major replaced it with a new kind of property tax. But the local authorities were demoralised still further by having to enforce two different taxes, both flawed, on the orders of central government. They still had one crucial responsibility, for schools, which they shared with the Department of Education; but in July 1992 the new Minister John Patten made it clear that he planned to remove schools completely from local councils.

Major's government has talked vaguely about decentralisation. The Minister for the Environment, Michael Howard, claims to be building bridges with local councils, and John Redwood, his Junior Minister in charge of local government, insists that councils are being given more responsibilities, for instance in community care – a thankless task. But the whole trend of government reforms – whether of police, fire brigades, schools or polytechnics – is towards removing responsibility from local councils, under the discipline of the 'capping' of local revenues by central grants which are based on the government's assessment of what councils need. The complaints about incompetent local councillors become self-fulfilling: the less the responsibility, the fewer first-class candidates will stand.

The British are now almost unique among western nations in the weakness of their local representation. They have been used to seeing

France as the most centralised nation, with roads, railways and decisions converging on Paris. But France's twenty-two regions now have their own governments chosen by direct elections since 1986, which have control over local institutions including secondary schools; and the once-powerful *Préfets* can no longer veto local decisions. Spain has gone through a more dramatic process of decentralising since Franco's death, which has given growing autonomy not only to the most demanding regions like Catalonia and the Basque Country, but to others like Castile who were not asking for it. The German *Länder* were given a federal structure after the Second World War, each with its own parliament and elections, as a safeguard against a resurgence of an over-powerful German state: but the competition between the regional capitals like Hamburg, Stuttgart and Munich soon added an extra vigour to the economic revival. In terms of smaller units, Switzerland provides the model of cantons which are protected by the constitution: 'as the most enduring confederation in the world, it has much to teach Europe,' says the former British Commissioner Christopher Tugendhat.

Governments in London like to point out that the European decentralised systems are much more expensive, and that large sums are wasted in bureaucratic overlap and official extravagance. But centralised governments can make very expensive mistakes (like subsidising Canary Wharf) by ignoring local conditions. London itself has no body which can act as a forum or a decisive centre for planning the capital. While the mayors of New York, Paris or Jerusalem are internationally known, the Lord Mayor of London is a figurehead, appointed each year to lead the ancient ceremonials of the City. 'We're the only country in Europe,' said Mark Fisher, the Labour shadow minister for arts in March 1992, 'without a democratic, strategic body to speak for its capital city.' And London is now the showplace, not only for central government, finance and conspicuous spending, but for every inner-city malaise – declining transport and services, poverty, homelessness and urban blight.

EUROPE OF CITIES

Provincial cities provide the most obvious focus for local pride and rivalry; ignored by London they look more towards Europe for their fulfilment and prospects. They see the main European cities vying with each other across the borders, for investment, for tourism, for industrial fairs and festivals. Many international investors, including multinational corporations, are more concerned with choosing the right city than the right nation. Provincial cities have looked back to their earlier history, before nation states took shape, when they were kingdoms, principalities or city states competing along the rivers and coastlines for trade and cultural glory. The old capitals of Eastern Germany are determined to rediscover their earlier internationalism, appealing directly to investors and donors abroad: when I visited Dresden in 1992 I was struck by its people's determination to reestablish their old reputation as the cultural capital of Eastern Germany, making the most of their superb opera house, art galleries and royal castle now lovingly being rebuilt. It is a trend of special interest to architects and town planners. In the words of the British-Italian architect Richard Rogers, who designed the Pompidou Centre in Paris and the Lloyd's building in London:

> We are witnessing in Europe the emergence of a new generation of cities. With the relative decline of the nation state, Europe is becoming increasingly defined by its cities. It is becoming, as it was until the seventeenth century, not a national but a city civilisation. And the reappearance of the city state has ushered in once again a very old and civilising European phenomenon – inter-city rivalry and competition.

The rich city-cultures of the continent provide better models for the British provinces than anything London can offer; while French or Dutch cities point to some solutions for British problems – whether for avoiding inner-city squalor, for planning traffic, underground systems and housing, or for achieving a better balance between public and private investments. The Channel Tunnel, when it is opened, will increase the rivalries and competitiveness between cities on both sides of the water; while the north and west of Britain will become more aware of the 'golden banana' that stretches in a crescent from Bristol to Barcelona.

SCOTLAND AND WALES

But the real puzzles in the British Constitution are the two regions Scotland and Wales (Northern Ireland which belongs to the United Kingdom but not Britain is outside the scope of this book). They have clearly suffered from the growing centralisation of power in London; but anyone who has watched the waxing and waning of regional protest over thirty years has to wonder: what is it really about?

The politicians have muddled it further, sometimes deliberately. Confusion was implicit in the vague word devolution, first used in Westminster politics in the 1880s during the debate on Home Rule for Ireland, to describe a compromise between Home Rule and direct rule. It became current again in the sixties, when the Labour government was unexpectedly threatened by nationalist movements in both Wales and Scotland. In 1966 the Welsh Nationalist Party Plaid Cymru, which had been founded in 1925, saw its first member in parliament; while the next year the Scottish Nationalist Party (SNP) – boosted by the discovery of oil off the Scottish shores – gained their first member, Winifred Ewing. The Labour cabinet appointed a Royal Commission on the Constitution under first Lord Crowther, and later Lord Kilbrandon, which failed to agree. The Conservatives in the meantime had promised a Scottish Assembly which they shelved when they returned to power in 1970. When Labour came back in 1974 they faced a worse threat, as the SNP won eleven seats and the Welsh three. Between them the nationalists now held the balance of power, and devolution was the price of their support. Labour introduced two Bills to give the regions Assemblies and greater autonomy, though without tax-raising powers; but when the Bills were put to a referendum neither region voted the necessary 40 per cent.

The regional crisis seemed to recede as suddenly as it had come; after the 1979 election the Scottish Nationalists retained only two seats, and Thatcher's government had less need for Scottish support. Under their policy of non-intervention they cut out regional grants and closed down major plants in Scotland. But in fact the Ministers for both Scotland and Wales were defying Thatcherism through development grants, and when Peter Walker became Secretary for Wales – which was meant as an insult and which it was assumed he would refuse – he became a dynamic intervener for Welsh interests, attracting major investors, particularly from Germany.

By the late eighties regional protest was brewing up again – particularly in Scotland, where Conservatives were losing votes to both Labour and the Scottish Nationalist Party; by 1987 they held only ten of the seventy-two seats in Scotland, and many Scots questioned their right to govern it. By the nineties separatism was surging again, with a groundswell which took London by surprise; and before the 1992 election the Tory hold on

Scotland looked tenuous. The Scottish Nationalists were excited by a poll in January which found that half the Scots wanted to become independent, and Murdoch's *Sun* stirred them up by supporting the SNP. John Major stood firm, and in his only heartfelt speech dwelt on the advantages of the union.

The election produced another Scots anticlimax. Plaid Cymru had increased from three to four, but the SNP still held only three seats (though they had increased their vote by 7 per cent). The Scots also now seemed less interested in independence (according to NOP) with only 28 per cent in favour of it, while 44 per cent supported a devolved assembly.

So what do the Scots really want? Their first need is proper recognition, both in London and the world beyond; but their bursts of assertion and anger appear to be more cultural and emotional than based on political and economic calculation. Secondly they need to escape from their sterile and introverted relationship with London. At present their interests are becoming still more interlocked with England as Scots and Welsh have both been disproportionately represented at Westminster, both in the Commons and in cabinets. Five of the twenty-two members of the Tory cabinet are of Scots origin; and a Welsh leader of the Labour Party has been followed by a Scot. The influence of Scots has been out of proportion to their numbers in finance, industry and specially in engineering where they have always excelled: but the road to promotion lies through London.

Centralisation of powers, and the weakening of alternative centres within Britain, makes some kind of Scots Assembly look attractive. The Scots are developing alternative links with other Europeans, to escape from the English embrace, and they already look to continental allies to support them against England; in football, when Germany plays England, they cheer Germany. More seriously, Scottish delegations have visited the provincial centres of Spain and Germany to observe their more effective autonomy, and Scots have closely followed the breakaways in Eastern Europe and the former Soviet Union, where the Baltic States and Croatia have joined the United Nations. The Scots do not want to compare themselves with the intolerant new tribal states of Eastern Europe or with 'ethnic cleansing': they prefer to find a parallel in Norway, with the same kind of population and oil, but with world recognition. And within the European Community they hope to reach a more productive balance between centralisation and autonomy.

EUROPE OF REGIONS

The idea of a 'Europe of Regions' was already current in the sixties; travelling through Europe in 1967, I became convinced of the need for stronger regional representation in the Community, to redress the power of central governments and reflect cultural identities. Since then the demands for local autonomy, like the Scots' demands, have waxed and waned, but they have been reinforced by the decentralising tendencies in France and Spain; and the Europe of Regions has become more convincing with the development of regional industries and tourism. All European nations, West and East, have faced more regional resentment since the end of the Cold War, and many regions have striven to identify themselves with the larger European context, rather than their own nation and capital. 'Europe is closer than Rome' is the slogan of the Lombardy League in Italy. 'Scotland will rejoin the world,' say the Scottish Nationalists. In Germany several *Länder* including Bavaria and Baden-Württemberg have complained that Bonn has worked too closely with Brussels in agreeing a common currency without local consultation.

The longing for local autonomy will not go away, whether on the continent or in Britain; and if Western Europe remains at peace, without a serious military threat from the East, the authority of the national capitals is likely to diminish. Defence justified centralised power, since weapons could only be organised and financed on a national scale. But regional consciousness grows with prosperity and peace: with the pursuit of cultural interests and diversity, with tourism and gastronomy, with the greater mobility of the car, and above all with the basic human need to put down local roots.

The ancient kingdoms and principalities of Europe still retain their cultural and political characteristics and rivalries, which they can often mobilise more constructively in the European context. They can forge their own collaborations across frontiers for trade, exchanges or common interests: the Mayor of Brest, for instance, has organised a club of seaports which includes Plymouth, Kiel and Cadiz.

But the future of any formal relationships between the regions and the Community remains unclear. The Maastricht Treaty allows for a 'Committee of Regions' to provide a presence in Brussels, which should have a 'common organisational structure' with the Economic and Social Committee. But the regions have no real powers in Brussels – not surprisingly. For the European Community was essentially constructed by nation states, under the firm control of the Council of Ministers who have no wish to have their powers eroded. The introduction of another layer of politicians and bureaucrats with separate access to Brussels could produce administrative chaos.

Regional development in Britain is still more uncertain, after the drastic undermining of local and city authorities in the eighties. Within England it is hard to discern a basis for serious regional breakaways: there is a wide gap between the romantic notions of ancient kingdoms like Mercia or Wessex, and the realities of economic dependence. At weekends I live a few miles from Wilton, which proclaims itself the ancient capital of Wessex, and there are occasional rumblings of nostalgia for Wessex man, encouraged by ancient ruins including Stonehenge and by the Marquess of Bath who long ago proclaimed himself King of Wessex. But the economy of Wiltshire is closely dependent on the motorway and train service to London, and its most booming town, Swindon, houses an outcrop of financial and other services which centre on the capital. Local opposition politicians dream of a revolt of the West Country, a reassertion of old liberalism or Celtic independence; but the votes at general elections follow the prevailing national swing.

Scotland and Wales remain distinctive, and are still able to defy economic forces in favour of cultural identity, with the help of their own languages. Centralisation in Westminster and Whitehall will continue to grow, which will add to their grievances. And the arguments for regional representation have become much stronger, not simply as a device to buy off angry demands for independence, but to break the inertia and deadlocks in the centre, so that (in the words of the Maastricht Treaty) 'decisions are taken as closely as possible to the citizen'.

15

Democracy in Crisis

'Decisions are taken as closely as possible to the citizen.' Many incoming prime ministers promise that ideal, but none achieve it. Mrs Thatcher saw herself as dismantling an inhuman socialist system, rolling back the frontiers of government and restoring individual liberties through free enterprise and choice. She certainly succeeded in cutting down the power of the trades unions, and liberating entrepreneurial energies. But she took drastic decisions affecting every citizen, with a minimum of consultation, which culminated in the fiasco of the poll tax. She replaced a small ruling circle with an even smaller one; and her successor has so far done little to widen the circle.

The gap between government and governed looms wider than ever, and Britain is run by one of the most centralised and least accountable systems in the industrial world. The complaint is familiar: a century ago Disraeli warned that 'centralisation is the death-blow of public freedom'; and across Europe there were clamours against centralising powers, particularly in France. But since the sixties the regions in France and elsewhere have successfully regained much initiative, while the British in the last decade have seen concentrations of power which the Victorians never dreamed of. The central control has tightened, and the countervailing powers outside Whitehall have been weakened. The Church, the Law, the universities and the monarchy have all lost influence. The middle ground of high-minded or non-political people, 'the great and the good', has been eroded. Town halls and provincial cities have been by-passed. Individual schools and hospitals may gain financial autonomy; but they are becoming accountable less to their locality, and more to Whitehall. Parliament, while proclaiming its sovereignty, allows still more decisions to be taken by the party-machines, the executive, the cabinet and the Council and Commission in Brussels.

The arena of power and influence has become narrower and bleaker since I first looked at Britain's anatomy thirty years ago, when a much more varied cast of characters crossed over the wide national stage: rough-hewn trades unionists, outspoken professors, eccentric scientists, indignant churchmen were all interrupting and contradicting the assumptions of Whitehall and the politicians' arguments at Westminster. Today the cast is much more conformist, on a stage largely restricted to London with sporadic noises off, mainly from the direction of Scotland. Professors and trades unionists are kept in the shadows. All the spotlights are trained on centre-stage, where a single party remains settled in power, with a monochrome background: mostly professionalised politicians with very limited experience outside parliament or the City.

The power at the centre, which Mrs Thatcher so rapidly increased through her personal domination, is far too great for any one person to wield effectively. The glare of media attention directed on Number Ten inevitably induces excessive expectations; but inside is a modest man who does not claim any bold vision of the country's future, and who more than his predecessors is a product of the market place, both political and economic, on which he depends. It was the financial markets that persuaded him as Chancellor to join the Exchange Rate Mechanism in October 1990; and it was the markets which forced him as prime minister to leave the Exchange Rate Mechanism in September 1992. (Ironically I had an appointment to interview the prime minister, to discuss some of the issues raised in this book, on the afternoon of September 16th. It had to be postponed just an hour beforehand – just when John Major was reaching the painful decision that he could no longer sustain Britain's basic economic policy.)

There is no very convincing alternative stage in the background, waiting to revolve; and the turnaround looks less likely than thirty years ago, when Harold Wilson was challenging Macmillan. The opposition remains for the time being divided and bewildered by the collapse of the earlier beliefs in socialism and nationalisation; and feel impelled to show that they, too, can sound like bank managers – depicting the whole world in terms of interest-rates, exchange rates and deficits. Without that central choice and difference of values between parties, other democratic choices also fall away. The British people have to depend still more heavily on general elections to give them their single moment of power; but the 1992 election effectively suppressed all the critical issues which were to dominate Britain for the rest of the year – whether the relationship with Europe, the exchange rate, the adjustment to the end of the Cold War, or the regulation of finance and big business.

In the business world the democracy of shareholders is as powerless as the democracy of voters in politics; while power in the boardrooms becomes more concentrated and less accountable. The liberation of finance in the eighties was supposed to put an end to any kind of corporate state and to introduce a new age of pluralism, with rival centres competing for influence like the financial cities of America. Instead a small group of London-based entrepreneurs have come much closer to Whitehall than they ever did under Labour. Global competition has justified the enlargement of a few British companies into a dominating size on a small island; and the bigger they are, the less shareholders can restrain their chairmen and directors from abuses, particularly from awarding each other salaries which make a mockery of pay restraint. Meanwhile the small businessmen, the heroes of the eighties, have become the chief casualties of recession, with little protection from the clout of the giants. At the top, the financial conglomerations converge with the political concentration in the charmed circle of mutual interests with strategic bargains – like the alliance between the Conservatives and the Murdoch media – which suit both sides at the expense of smaller groupings and dissenting voices.

The wielders of power at the top create their own dangerous illusions: for they are more interdependent with other nations and interests than they care to tell the public. Britain's sovereignty has always been exaggerated: in defence she lost much of her independence when she joined Nato forty-five years ago, while in finance her limitations were exposed when the IMF dictated Britain's budget in 1976. But when Britain joined the European Community in 1972 she was committed to the slower, deeper processes of joint decisions, compromises and constraints – which were never spelt out in the White Paper's promise: 'no question of any erosion of essential national sovereignty.' As the processes continued, both ministers and civil servants became interlocked with their counterparts in Brussels in negotiations which were still more distant from their citizens; and they offered no explanation. The Community has affected nearly every centre of British power, gradually and often imperceptibly, like the 'incoming tide' which Lord Denning described: changing levels and horizons while retaining the structures. Whitehall, Westminster and the Law Courts look the same, but Europe has created a higher court in the Law, challenged monopolies, protected the environment. And diplomats, mandarins and judges have gradually come to terms with the wider context.

The public had little chance to adjust; for governments remained fearful of a popular backlash, and did not try to educate them. Britain joined Europe not in a fit of absence of mind, as she was said to have acquired her Empire, but by a process of deliberate deception. Twenty years later the public is beginning to realise some of the consequences; but will face many more shocks in the future. Today most people regard Margaret Thatcher as the prime minister who has most changed Britain over the post-war decades; but future historians may well choose Ted Heath, who brought Britain into a European process from which it could not be extricated.

The economic links with Europe went ahead much more rapidly than the public awareness. The British joined the Exchange Rate Mechanism in October 1990, which bound them to the other central banks, without any correspondingly close relationship with political institutions. It suited the government to have an external discipline to maintain the fight against inflation, and to use the strength of the Deutschmark to support the pound – as earlier governments had used the gold standard. But the Bundesbank had to be exceptionally harsh because the colossal cost of German reunification required vast borrowing which pushed up interest-rates. (It would have been much less harsh if Bonn had increased taxes to pay for East Germany, but that was against Conservative philosophy.) When the pound weakened and fell out of the Exchange Rate Mechanism it was all too easy to blame the Bundesbank for being insensitive, but insensitivity was their duty as defenders of their currency: and it was the strength of the Deutschmark which was the chief attraction of the ERM.

Britain in any case was dependent on the Bundesbank because of its involvement in European trade, whether inside or outside the Community. Businessmen and bankers, rather than politicians, had first brought the continent closer together. European nations in the late twentieth century could be compared to the American states in the late nineteenth century, when railroads, oil pipelines and banks were forging structures across the continent which enabled giant companies to sell the same products from coast to coast. The state legislatures, inward-looking and often corrupt, were slow to realise what was hitting them, and when the farmers of the west lost their money in the recession they attacked the eastern bankers and the gold standard with eloquent but helpless fury: 'you shall not crucify mankind upon a cross of gold.' It was not until half a century later, under F. D. Roosevelt, that Washington developed effective powers to limit and regulate the big corporations and banks, and the Federal government became dominant.

The United States already had a federal constitution to build on, and a people with a common experience of emigration, revolution and independence. Europe's nations have a much longer history than America's states, with less common culture and no common language; so Europeans can less easily accept, or adapt to, a federal or confederal structure. But Europe faced a similar challenge in the fifties when financial and commercial interests romped across their continent; and their need for a customs union played a decisive role in pushing through the Treaty of Rome. Businessmen were the first to become supranational, followed reluctantly by politicians and diplomats. It is this time-lag which has caused the 'democratic deficit' – the bleak phrase which itself suggests that everything can be measured in money.

The British with their insular tradition found new European political institutions harder to accept than most continentals who in spite of past enmities shared traditions of the law, strong bureaucracies and state regulation. British governments enjoyed depicting the European Commission as a 'monster' (John Major) or a 'politburo' (Margaret Thatcher). And it is certainly an undemocratic and unaccountable body with no real separation of powers, ruled by expatriate civil servants doubly removed from their own people. But governments frequently use the Commission as a diversion from the real European power, the Council of Ministers which represents the governments themselves. It is the Council which conducts the secret horse-trading and bargaining, and which makes proposals for the Commission to execute. And the decisions of both bodies have raced ahead of democratic control.

The Treaty of Maastricht and the crisis of the Exchange Rate Mechanism brought all the dangers of an undemocratic Europe to a head. The Treaty, which has little to do with agriculture, became the target of German and French farmers in the regions who saw themselves threatened by a strict single currency and high interest-rates – echoing the anger of American farmers a century ago who protested against the 'cross of gold'. And the Exchange Rate Mechanism became the scapegoat for every European government's determination to cut back inflation. British workers, who faced a deeper recession and higher unemployment, were inclined to blame the faceless bureaucrats of Brussels. In fact the Community's Social Chapter is much more sympathetic to their needs than the British government's.

To turn back from the European political process would only make

Britain more helpless against the underlying movements of finance and industry. Even right outside the Community, like Sweden, Britain would find her prosperity and currency heavily dependent on the Deutschmark and the Bundesbank. And if the British tried to halt their progress into Europe they would stop any prospect of a more democratic balance, and retreat back into a more dangerously insular mentality.

For Europeans have a far richer and more varied contribution to make to each other than is suggested by the bleak processes of harmonisation, regulation and horse-trading in Brussels. The crisis of the exchange rates has revealed all the narrowness of the current idea of Europe, as all the splendours and contrasts of the continent are viewed through the dealing-room floor, and French farmers or shopkeepers suddenly appear on television, only because of their attitude to Maastricht. The real benefit of Europe for Britain lies in the escape from an introverted island, into a wider and more open society, stimulated by closer contact and competition with other peoples. Thirty years ago Macmillan saw it clearly enough when he said: 'It is a cold shower we enter, not a Turkish bath.' Iain Macleod was privately more emphatic: 'If Britain doesn't join Europe, she will become like Portugal.' But the opening-up took much longer than either expected; and now it is Portugal that is being revived by Europe, much more than Britain.

Looking back over thirty years at Britain's institutions – whether schools, law-courts, engineering institutions or banks – I see them still trapped in closed circles: they frustrate any attempts at reform as they turn in on themselves. The schools still do not equip Britons with the languages and knowledge to move confidently in the contemporary world, particularly on the continent. The media are still preoccupied with the English-speaking world and remain caught up with a mutual love-affair with parliament which prefers to ignore Europe. The Law still cannot connect up with a European convention which provides stronger human rights for the citizen. Yet in the meantime many adventurous young Britons are finding fulfilment on the continent and beyond: academics escaping from back-biting high tables, engineers discovering a more respected profession or businessmen looking for more enterprising customers. Even ordinary tourists discover that the French, Germans or Italians can help to teach Britain how to run railways, education or cities.

The British remain rightly proud of their democratic continuity; yet they are easily misled by their fear of continental state systems. For many of their treasured traditions – whether of the common law, local government, or self-regulation – have proved inadequate to stand up to the centralising power of their own state; and they cannot effectively defend citizens against creeping bureaucracies, or against unscrupulous crooks like Maxwell. While British politicians relish their unique history of freedom, their voters have to look to Strasbourg as their ultimate protector.

The structure of the European Community retains a fatal flaw – the lack of accountability to its citizens. It is not just a 'democratic deficit' but a lack of the life-blood of argument and dissent – which is all too obvious in the hermetic atmosphere and language of Brussels. Jean Monnet, the founder of the Community, wanted to democratise Europe through developing a strong parliament, and wanted Britain to show the way. But British voters and politicians refused to take the European parliament seriously, which weakened their own democracy as their government became more centralised and more interlocked with Europe's.

The British still have more democratic instincts than most Europeans, as many leaders including Mitterrand have freely admitted. They still insist on arguing proposed changes before they legislate; while too often the others first approve and then complain – or simply ignore the rules. But British politics are stuck in the wrong scale, discussing the wrong problems. The election campaign of 1992 revealed all the limitations of the political debate. The parties argued about details of taxes and the health service, and the media revelled in the daily television spectacular, while they all conspired to ignore the wider issues, including the monetary system and the Maastricht Treaty which would affect everyone's lives. Four months later the new government watched the Treaty crashing down around them, and the crisis of the European exchange rates became the over-riding political issue.

There is now a deadly disconnection between serious policies and democracy – in Britain as elsewhere in Europe. The Community has to be democratised, or disintegrate. The Maastricht Treaty and the move towards a common currency remain essential goals; but they cannot be implemented without fundamental democratic oversight and controls. The task is not impossible: the European parliament can be reconstructed to provide a formidable counter to Brussels, questioning Commissioners, investigating their decisions and if necessary firing them. But the ghostly set-up in Strasbourg betrays all the symptoms of an institution imposed from above – while the real revolts are brewing up elsewhere, from below.

The furious explosions against the Maastricht Treaty and currencies can yet provide the shock necessary to transform this moribund chamber. But it has to be far more closely linked to the national parliaments, to give it legitimacy and democratic roots; and particularly with Westminster – which has been the most obstructive and jealous.

British members of parliament will have to face up to their responsibilities and limitations: for their own people are now so under-represented that they are seriously concerned about the Constitution for the first time since the Second World War – as the success of the lobby Charter 88 bears witness. The British government attacks the monster in Brussels as a decoy from its own centralising policies at home; but the national and continental trends are both linked to the financial concentrations of power. They call out for scrutiny at every level – continental, national and local – and for a democratic movement to implement the promise at Maastricht: that 'decisions are taken as closely as possible to the citizen.'

It is absurd that this critical objective should be described by the ugly word subsidiarity (first used by the Pope in 1931, in reference to Christian doctrine) – with its associations with subsidence and subsidy which both convey what Lord Scarman calls 'that sinking feeling'. For subsidiarity is just what Britain urgently needs to escape from over-centralisation at home. As Scarman describes it:

> It is not a delegation of power downwards but a sharing of the distribution of the power of government so as to achieve a close relation between those who govern and those who are governed. It is a principle which can increase the people's participation in government.[1]

There is no contradiction between strengthening Europe and forging stronger regional and local units. The competition between regions for investment, between cities for festivals, fairs or special grants, or between local councils for subsidies from Brussels, are all providing different levels of contact across Europe; while the continental dimension can help to defuse the most explosive resentments of regions against their national capitals, by-passing them to treat directly with each other or with Brussels.

The British are less equipped to decentralise their political power than

[1] Lord Scarman: Why Britain Needs a Written Constitution, Sovereignty Lecture for Charter 88, July 20, 1992.

most Europeans: for their local leadership has been dominated and demoralised by central government. Yet the government cannot make public services more accountable, whether through a Citizen's Charter or through other means, without first giving citizens a closer sense of local participation, enabling them to complain to local hospitals, school authorities or railway stations with some prospect of redress. Governments have to face up to the problems of sharing power, both at the bottom with local authorities, and at the top with other Europeans, and to open up their decisions to public inspection. They cannot resolve the crisis of democracy and representation within their own borders: too many of the roads lead off the map, towards Brussels, Frankfurt or Washington. There is never an end to the pursuit of 'the will-o'-the-wisp of power' as Aneurin Bevan called it, as I have found in trying to anatomise Britain: modern society is so complex that decisions always seem to be taken somewhere else. But no democracy can be effective unless the public is allowed to know how and where decisions are taken, and given some sense of participation. The British must recognise that they are already governed by many European forces beyond their control; but they cannot move further towards the Community without a far more effective parliamentary supervision and counter-power.

Index

INDEX

Shultz, George, 140
Simon, David, 116
Simpson, John, 128
Single European Treaty, 15
Small businesses, 119–20, 156
Smith, John, 27–8, 30
  and trades unions, 138
Social Democrat Party, 30
Sovereignty, 53, 156
Spain, decentralisation, 148
Sports on television, 131
Standard of living, 141
State schools, 67–71
Sterling, Jeffrey, Lord Sterling
  (P & O), 84, 110, 121
Stewart, William, 78
Stirling, Angus, 66
Stock Exchange, 101
Strage, Henry M., 114–15
Strathalmond, Lord, 115
Students, 64–76
Subsidiarity, 161
Swindon, new industry, 106
Switzerland, cantons, 148

Taylor, Lord, Lord Chief Justice, 47
Teachers and Government, 65
Television, 127–32
  ITV, 19–32
  of Parliament, 10–11
Thames TV, 129, 130
Thatcher, Margaret, Lady Thatcher,
  154, 157
  and BBC, 127, 128
  cabinet, 19–20, 64
  and centralisation of power, 155
  and Channel Tunnel, 83
  and Church of England, 55
  and the City, 87
  and Civil Service, 33, 34, 37, 39
  and Defence staff, 41
  and EC, 6, 15, 45, 158
  fall, 10, 20, 110

and Foreign Office, 43
and General Election 1992, 1, 2
and ITV, 129
on individualism, 11
and industrialists, 121–2
and local government, 147
and John Major, 20, 21
and monarchy, 58
monetarism, 40
and Open University, 72
snubbed at Oxford University, 77
and Parliament, 11–12
and peerage, 54
poll tax, 147
as President, 61–2
privatisation policy, 108, 109–10
and Royal Commissions, 75
and science, 77, 78
and small businesses, 119
and transport, 111
unemployment under, 140, 141
and unions, 136, 137, 138
Thomson, Lord (IBA), 129
Todd, Ron (TGWU), 139
Trades Union Congress, 134–5, 138
  and Europe, 135, 138–9
Trades unions see Unions
Training, 64–5
Transport, privatisation, 111–12
Transport and General Workers
  Union (TGWU), 138
Travellers, 143–4
Treasury, 38–41
Trevi Committee, 38
Tugendhat, Sir Christopher, 148
Tumim, Stephen, Judge, 49
Tutu, Archbishop Desmond, 58
TV AM, 129

Unemployment, 140–2
  graduate, 71
  and unions, 136, 140
Unilever, 14